About the author

Ian Foxley was born in Gwent in 1956 and is the third of seven siblings. After an exciting career in the Army, he became IT Director for Domino's Pizza UK and Ireland before running his own franchises and then embarking on his third career as a writer and bon-vivant. He has contributed to an anthology of comical essays and is currently writing Television and film scripts and acting as military technical advisor to the film industry.

He is an ex- rugby player, qualified referee and coaches mini-rugby in his local rugby club at Malton and Norton RUFC. He lives in York and still enjoys a wide range of sports and is constantly surprised that he has time to do anything else at all. He is married with three children aged, 7, 13 and 15 who keep him busy and young at heart.

Charity Registration No. 295672

Granting wishes of children aged 3 to 18 living with life-threatening illnesses

A donation will be made to Make-A-Wish Foundation® UK, for every copy sold of this edition of Educating Daddy.

Educating Daddy

Ian Foxley

Bentwyck Henry Publishers

Published by   Bentwyck Henry Publishers Ltd
36 Hart Street
Henley-on-Thames
Oxfordshire
RG 9 2AU, England
National 01491 413100
International (+44) 1491 413100
E-mail: bentwyckhenrybks@aol.com
Website: www.bentwyckhenry.co.uk

ISBN 1-904538-12-6

Ian Foxley has asserted his moral right under the Copyright, Designs and Patents Act 1988 to be identified as the author of this work.

Typeset in Apple Garamond and Sand

Printed and Bound in Great Britain by
Antony Rowe Ltd, Chippenham, Wiltshire

Cover Design by DNA Design Consultants

A copy of this book is held at the British Library

Disclaimer: The term 'tweenies used within this book is a collective term used to describe the age group of children BETWEEN Infancy and Teens. No link is inferred or suggested with the commercial term 'Tweenies' which is a registered trademark of the British Broadcasting Corporation used to describe a group of puppets/mannequins.

Acknowledgements

First and foremost, my thanks go to a seven year old domestic terrorist called Nicholas who is currently living in our house and who keeps asking me awkward questions about why the sky is blue, where God lives and what happens when things die. My responses are normally followed by a detailed interrogation to determine how and where Daddies learn such facts. Thus, the invention of Daddy's College: the fantasy institution that Daddies go to in order to learn the things that Daddies need to know. This in turn led to the need to write this book to show him, and others like him, that Daddy's College really could exist in order to answer the multitude of questions springing from an enquiring young mind. My further thanks go to those honorary graduates of Daddy's College - our fantasy institution for educating fathers - and to all the home-tutored Mums who have added their wisdom over the past year with patience, wonder and kind-heartedness. Of particular note are these assorted Mums and Dads: Tim and Claire Blenkin, Julian and Laura Boddy, John and Jo Denton, Scott and Nicki Ewing, Gordon and Jocelyn Foxley, Richard and Ann Hill, Clare and Joe Horsley, Jennifer Hornyak, Karen Ilsley, Jenny Kent, Jim and Gillian Kelsey, Alan Latham and Helen Torlesse, Gary and Michelle Lineker, John and Katherine Norling, David and Shelley Ross, John and Gillian Ross, David and Belinda Sheppard, Daphne Taylor, Justin and Paula Tomlin-Kent, Tom and Amanda Welch and a host of others who have not scorned my idiocy but gently pointed me in the right direction with a glass of milk and a biscuit. I would like to add my particular thanks to Comfort Bingham, my Publisher, and Jon Lake, editor, for their belief, patience and support in getting my words and thoughts from crazed madness into print in a readable form. Posthumous thanks are owed to H.Rider Haggard for the term 'SHE who must be obeyed' from his classic novel of the same name, a term for the 'Mummy-People' that is not used perjoratively but in true recognition of the realities of domestic life. And, of course, I owe very special thanks to Emma, who is Freddie, Jessica and Nicholas' very own Mummy, without whose constant support I would be merely a sad man, and not a happy Daddy.

IF... you want to be a Good Daddy

If you can keep your children all about you
When others, losing theirs, just envy you,
If you can trust yourself when your wife doubts you
And make allowance for her mother too,
If you can wait all night and not mind waiting,
Until your darling daughter's safely home,
Yet teach your sons the Rules of Proper Dating,
To care for girls, as sisters of their own:

If you can dream for every son and daughter,
Then help them realise their hopes and dreams;
If you can play their games in sand and water
Yet still be friends when they are in their teens;
If you have ridden Triumphs and gone faster
Than you would really want your child to go,
Yet treat them kind when they should meet Disaster,
By dealing your new car a body blow:

If you can make one heap of all your earning
And watch it spent on food and clothes and shoes,
Or wonder how you'll pay for all their learning
Yet keep an open mind to all their views;
If you can force your heart and nerve to let you
Hold back while Little People risk their all,
In trying things their Mother wouldn't want to
Yet still be there to catch them when they fall:

If you can tell them tales and show them wonders
Of all you've seen and done in your short time,
Whilst stopping them from making all your blunders,
Yet help them grow and push their boundary line;
If you can show them how to fill their minutes
With sixty seconds' worth of work and fun,
Then Theirs will be the Earth and all that's in it,
And you'll have done a Father's job. Well done!

Lyrics by Ian Foxley to a tune by Rudyard Kipling

Contents

Foreword
by Gary Lineker

Could it be a back-handed compliment to be asked to write a foreword for *Educating Daddy*? Is there something that good friends are trying to say but no one dare? Has my parental deodorant failed? No, I am assured, even though the Lineker's domestic Chief Examiner, aka the lovely Mrs Lineker, is holding back my final scorecard until our youngest is 18 years old, she has predicted that I might qualify for my very own Daddy's College Graduation Certificate and Tee shirt if I practise Chapters 1-8 on our children and learn Chapter 9 by heart.

This is an amusing book, which leads old, young and prospective Dads onto the playing field of fatherhood, whilst offering useful hints on how best to avoid being blown up for being 'Offside' or getting a parental yellow card. I enjoyed doing the exercises and homework which I found, surprisingly, both fun to do and provocative in making me assess my thoughts and actions as a Dad. I particularly love the concept of Daddy's Tax, especially when it comes to crisps...

Educating Daddy is also committed to supporting the Make-A-Wish Foundation ® UK, a charity which grants wishes for children aged 3 to 18 living with life-threatening illnesses. Having experienced at first-hand the horrific trauma and difficulties of having a child burdened by a potentially fatal disease, as our eldest, George, was by leukaemia, we understand how much a charity like the Make-A-Wish Foundation ® UK can help provide some joy and fun in an otherwise uncompromising situation. As one of the Blinding Glimpses of the Obvious in this book observes "Your children won't learn about charity unless they see you practise it!" So, even if paternal pride leads a Dad to believe that he can't learn anything from *Educating Daddy*, you are at least helping to support a worthwhile charity with every copy that you purchase – so get one for every man you know.

What comes out of this compendium is the conclusion that Dads everywhere really do need a Daddy's College as a source of helpful, practical advice to help them with the hardest task for any man in the world – that of being a good Dad. After all, children don't come with operating instructions and if we can get our generation of Dads to do their job well, then our children will have a really good head start in learning how to be great Mums and Dads to our grandchildren.

Gary Lineker, May 2005

A brief word from a well-known father

Ho ho ho ! So you're a father. Well, take it from somebody who's been one for a very long time now, it's going to change your life in such ways that you'll wonder why nobody warned you about it beforehand - and in the strongest possible terms. The second thing you'll notice is how little you know about the process of being a Dad. I see lots of children in my annual travels and, year after year, I am constantly amazed by how these blank little canvasses so closely reflect the paint strokes laid by their parents. A moving masterpiece can be created in the most unlikely of places through the care, attention and wisdom of parental artists, regardless of social standing, wealth or creed.

Equally, I have seen, and feel for, the lost potential of those who will never have the chance to be admired in the human gallery because of the failure of their elders to use the parental palette properly. Remember it is you who holds the brush and it is you who will sketch the outline for your children to colour in the detail. By following the advice in this Handbook, I believe that you will have

the opportunity to create your own masterpieces – or at least sketch a jolly good cartoon for the future. Good luck, and I'll see you mid-winter for a mince pie, a glass of sherry and a chat with Mummy to see how you and the children are getting on.

Introduction

"How the heck do I deal with this?"

There are going to be (at least) three major occasions when you, as a Dad, are going to pause for thought and wonder how to approach the immediate paternal problem confronting you. The first occasion will be when you hold your first-born child in your arms, and it does something that you've never really experienced before: possibly smelly, probably noisy and definitely bewildering. The second occasion will follow about seven years later when, seemingly out of nowhere, the same little chap (or chappess) ambushes you with one of the 'Sacred Mysteries': "Where does God live?" "What happens to us when we die?" or "Why are the sky and the sea blue?" The third major occasion will come about ten years later as the selfsame big chap innocently asks you whether their girlfriend/boyfriend can stay overnight and will it be OK if they sleep in the same room?

The Need for a Book Like 'Educating Daddy'

Welcome to the minefield of issues that are going to confront you almost every day for the rest of your life. These are the 'joys' of fatherhood. It would be great if all men came with an instruction Handbook, but when they become Dads it actually becomes a necessity. How else do men learn how to be Dads? Dads are no longer just the major breadwinner, absent all day at work and present only at home in the evenings and weekends to give the most minimal input to parenting. More and more modern Dads are working from home or are following alternative careers that allow them more time with their families and greater input as a Dad. Thus, a Handbook for Dads is becoming a necessity to help with the daily complexities of close contact with Mum and the Kids.

Indeed, a number of recent studies (see annexes) show such uncomfortable trends in modern society that we can no longer go on assuming that all is well with fatherhood. Family structures and the traditional roles of Mums and Dads have changed over the past thirty years, with 75% of households now having dual incomes and the number of full-time working Mums with pre-school children has doubled. More families than ever are single parent families and fewer than ever co-habit as a cohesive tri-generation unit.

However, whilst traditional roles might have changed, male perceptions haven't. The number of men in employment and their total hours worked per week may have fallen but working Mums still put twice the number of hours into housework than working Dads and our Family Court system is still grossly skewed in favour of mothers rather than fathers. The effect on the current generation of children is also worrying. There has been a 30% rise in births to unmarried mothers since 1976 whilst a greatly increased adolescent use/abuse of drugs and alcohol has seen a consequent rise in the juvenile crime rate and a lowering of participation in the adult labour force. More teenage girls suffer from anorexia or bouts of self-inflicted harm - often related to a distant or punitive parental relationship. Many have a lowering of general self-esteem and a greater reliance on social welfare programmes in a fruitless search for the ultra-slim, Ok! Magazine, luxury workless lifestyle.

On the other hand, positive father involvement in family life has been shown to directly improve exam results, to improve school attendance, and reduce criminality, while resulting in better quality interpersonal relationships and good mental health in children. Men who do more housework have wives who want more sex and their children do much better both socially and academically. Moreover, the effect of such active participation spills over into the wider social family, as fathers accept their responsibility to act as male role models and help shape and control the actions and behaviour of the next generation, not merely those of their own children.

Given that fatherhood is such a common occurrence, and one which has been going on globally for such a long time, it is frankly amazing that more has not been written on the subject and that the shelves of libraries and bookshops are not stacked with helpful tomes offering advice to current and prospective fathers. Certainly, there are forests of Good Parenting books for Mums, but if you try searching for one written specifically for ordinary men who just want a helpful guide on how to be a good Dad, then you are facing a more difficult task, and you may still be perusing the shelves when your offspring are asking for the car keys.

How the heck do I deal with this?

Who Should Read it?

'Educating Daddy' is targeted specifically at Dads. It has a number of serious messages, which are dealt with in a manner likely to stimulate and amuse the intelligent male mind. Hopefully, the female reader will also find it an invaluable prompt for the main man in her family life. In an ideal world, prospective Dads would seek out such a book for themselves knowing that they are going to need some form of reference over the coming years. In the real world, it is likely that the first person reading this introduction will be an expectant Mum, a current Mum, a concerned Grandma or some other caring friend who knows a husband, son or dad who needs a helping hand. Or it might perhaps be a wife, mother, child or friend seeking an amusing but helpful present which may be given at any time throughout the year in answer to the question: "What can I get Dad that he hasn't got already?" If this person is you, dear prospective purchaser and/or reader, please remember that this book has been written for him to read as a Dad, not as a husband or as a single man and, whilst there may be many things that all men in general need to know, this volume is intended to be a useful handbook written by a Dad, for other Dads.

Is the content suitable for a Dad ?

We asked a host of mums the question 'What are the top five things you want your man to know as a Dad?' Their answers were stitched into the fabric of the book and are, in some cases, the source of inspiration for the cartoons. Interestingly, none of the mums mentioned "how to warm or sterilise a bottle or burp the baby". They were far deeper in that what they wanted a Dad to know was how to balance what they knew as Mums and to fill in what they, as men, were perceived to have overlooked or had not even thought about as Dads. The subject has been approached in a deliberately light manner that coats a serious message beneath. Knowing how men hate to be patronised themselves, I have tried not to adopt too earnest a tone, or too proscriptive a *diktat* which I believe would distract most men rather than interest and amuse them. Whilst I have tried not to be vomit-worthily mawkish, I do note that it is still an honourable thing to love and care for your children, take an interest in what they want to be in life and try to help them on their way.

What's NOT in the book

The book is slim not because I ran out of words when I sent the manuscript for publishing, but because a thumping great tome that dissects fatherhood down to its minutiae will probably just be guaranteed a dusty place on the spare room windowsill. Better by far to produce what becomes a well-thumbed and useful guide kept handily in the downstairs loo, and dipped into regularly. There was a great (commercial) temptation to write a book targeting only prospective or new Dads; such a book would have been easier to pen and quicker to get into print, but would have done a great disservice to all those Dads for whom the new problems that arise as children get older are no less real and no less perplexing. So, I have tried to include all the major topics that Dads are likely to need but have not hammered them to death. If you need to know how to change a nappy or deal with siblings, look in the forest of self-help books for Mums – the contents won't change just because it's a man reading it!

Layout of the Book

The first three parts of the book correspond to the major developmental stages of your child. A fourth part deals with serious issues that affect children of all ages. Remember that no child sticks to a rigid development timetable, therefore some of the information in one section may overlap in your particular experience. The groupings follow traditional patterns still found in most tribal communities in the Third World where children live in their Mother's House for the first seven years, their Father's House for the next seven years and then progress on puberty into the House of their Guardian or Mentor. The book is similarly divided into these major periods:

Part One, **'The Primary Years'**, deals with the transition from safe, secure bachelorhood and Dinky (Double Income No Kids Yet) existence into the trauma of imminent fatherhood, infancy and the early years, with dependant 'Leg Limpets' – babes in arms, toddlers, and children aged up to about seven.

Part Two, **'The Middle Ages'**, focuses on the intermediate or 'in between' years with 'tweenie children in that awkward stage between infancy and the teenage years. Your child will be turning its primary focus from its mother to you, as a father, for a whole range of guidance, direction and support.

Part Three, **'Senior Students'**, projects you forward through the Teenage Time Tunnel where you will face the challenges posed by what we call 'Gangly Lions', children who have reached that most awkward, hormone-fuelled stage. You will have to sort out their education and career planning and finally off-load your loved ones so that they do NOT remain KIPPERS (Kids in Parents' Pockets Eating Up Retirement Savings), all while facing the many challenges of young adult rebellion.

Part Four, **'Family Matters'** deals with issues that you are likely to come accross whether your offspring are Leg Limpets, 'tweenies or Gangly Lions. The nature of this material means that this part is rather more reflective and laden with gravitas. However, light refreshment follows in the annexes where you will find useful summaries, your scorecard and a graduation certificate if you have followed the Course within the book.

Oops !....

If you believe that I have missed some vital aspect of fatherhood or wish to forward ideas for inclusion, (whether you're a Dad or a Mum), or if you have some particular experience that would be of benefit to other student Dads then please assist us by using the Internet link at www.educatingdaddy.com or www.daddyscollege.com All identities will be closely guarded and any inclusion in future editions will be at the discretion of the author (and his lawyers).

No offence is meant to any particular organization, group, sexual proclivity, political stance, colour, creed, or religion. Undoubtedly, there will be many who will object to my treatises on paternal behaviour and declare me utterly incompetent to voice opinions on the elements of domestic politics, social anthropology, home economics or metaphysical cosmology found herein. To them, I wholly admit to my inability to worship at the altar of multi-tasking maternal perfection But I hold by my Charter that all Men have the right to be good Daddies in order to illuminate their way through the darkness to achieve peace with their partners and friendship with their offspring.

The Student Dad

The book takes the form of a textbook used within 'Daddy's College' - an imaginary educational institution created for current and prospective fathers (Student Dads). The chapters offer advice, **Blinding Glimpses of the Obvious**, Exercises and, of course, Homework. Some of the exercises are for completion with wives/partners and are designed not only to illuminate, but also to raise important issues for you to discuss if you ever get the chance to talk sensibly together again once you've had children. Even if you are appalled at the idea of having to complete this Coursework, try it in the safe knowledge that SHE will wholly approve of your interest and participation in learning about parenting. If you find suggestions that you don't like then please feel free to ignore them. Whilst I would like you to try new practices, if something really doesn't appeal to you then don't torture yourself with guilt, just allow your wife to do that for you when she finds out that you have skipped a few exercises. Note that Mums, as the appropriate local Chief Examiners, can monitor the progress of their particular students through a checklist in the Annexes to ensure that homework is not shirked. A Graduation Certificate has been included for issue to good boys – just make sure you get a playtime bonus when SHE issues it.

I do not profess to have all the answers, and this book is not meant to be a universal compendium. It is not immersed in psychobabble nor born from 'fashionable' new theories. Rather, it is founded on common sense and those practical solutions that appear to work.

The 'Government Health Warning'

Stamped indelibly into all pages of the book is the warning that nothing written here is guaranteed to work for you and your children. In fact, even though it might work for one of them it might not work for another. Children are individuals made up from a pot-pourri of genetic inheritance, environmental influence and learned experience. Each is different and each will need different ways and means to bring out their best aspects and develop their best potential. Indeed, I do note that our own children are still in the moulding pot and, if some bright young literary critic hopes to make his/her name by declaiming my advice based on the evidence of my own children then I wish him/her all the best: he/she can borrow them for the school holidays to see if they can do any better. I merely hope to show you the armoury at your disposal, and to offer you the opportunity to use the appropriate tools at about the right point in time. It is you who will wield them to mould your children for the future. Enjoy the read, study well, and graduate with honour because you're going to be tested in each of these areas by a Little Person who won't take 'NO' for an answer - and remember, his/her Mummy will be watching too..... May the beer go with you.

Part One - The Primary Years

A guide to 'Leg Limpets' for the new Dad

Educating Daddy

Part One
The Primary Years
'Leg Limpets'

These early chapters are for the new father. For the proud new 'owner' of a baby or 'Leg Limpet', that small and utterly dependant new life that might once have seemed to be an uncommunicative bundle of bodily functions, but which you will soon see as something wonderful and miraculous.

The shock of impending fatherhood may still be cushioned by a warm glow of pride that emanates from the inward recognition that your investment in condoms, throughout your wild bachelor days was worth it after all. If however, you feel totally unprepared and overwhelmed for it, then welcome to the club! Parenthood will demand unexpected and unacknowledged depths of psychological and emotional adjustment in the months and years to come. Up until now, babies will have been things that other men have which change them from normal football/rugby/squash playing/watching mates who are up for a boys' night out into pre-occupied, impoverished, party-poopers. Once normal blokes who now automatically gravitate towards other fathers to exchange stories of sleepless nights and houses that smell of poo.

Very soon, you too will be regaling the world at large with a whole new universe of emotions and experiences at which you have hitherto scoffed Enjoy the euphoria for a few moments, because we have to get down to the serious stuff of how you are going to cope with it, what changes you are going to have to make and most importantly, how you're going to pay for it. Apologies to those of you for whom this is 'Old Hat': you should recognize the truth in these statements, and will smile knowingly as a *paternal cognoscenti*, having already transformed in varying degrees of success from carefree DINKY to harassed Dad. Even if you are no longer worrying about how to change a nappy or whether you'll pass muster parade when the Health Visitor arrives for her first inspection, you should also find the odd gem herein.

You may have been bought this Handbook by one of the ladies in your life who loves you dearly and who hopes and expects that you will become one of the best Dads in the world to your children. We hope that the chapters and exercises in this book will help you accomplish that aim.

Educating Daddy

1

Darling, We're Pregnant!
How to cope with the bombshell

OK, so how do YOU feel?

Your life-changing moment will start when you hear the immortal words: "Darling, we're pregnant", or some similarly-phrased bombshell. This will be dropped as a casual remark, although your wife / partner will have spent hours quietly working out exactly how, precisely when and just where you will best receive it. How you feel about this bombshell will depend on a number of different factors, going far beyond your state of sobriety and whether or not your favourite team are winning when you hear the news:

a) Your personal experience and personality

How were you brought up? Did your parents take a great part in your young life or were they experiencing a difficult time in their own relationships that had an impact on you? Did you have lots of brothers and sisters or were you an only child? Did you have a 'happy childood' or were you desperate to get away? These experiences will affect your feelings towards your impending offspring and, most importantly, what you want to do for it. The two main questions are: do you actually want to be a Dad and do you feel that you're ready for it? The answer to the first question is normally "Yes", accompanied by a smug pride that your bollocks actually work as advertised. The answer to the second question is very often "No", accompanied by a naïve belief that nothing is really going to change anyway. We have no ready answers for any of these questions - only you can ascertain your true feelings about them. An early warning here - be VERY careful about how you broach any of the answers with your wife/partner because SHE will also have a completely different set of experiences, distorted by an unpredictable and invisible surge in maternal hormones which could drive her to react in a very different manner.

b) The current state of your relationship

Have you been together for a long time? Have you cemented your relationship in marriage, or are you still 'carefree spirits from Hippyville surfing the tide of time on a stormy sea of life', or perhaps you are desperately trying to fix a failing relationship and hope that a child will bring you closer together? If so, then you might well be feeling anxious, uncertain or even slightly worried that your new child will somehow distract your partner from you and unsettle your relationship together. Whatever your answers to these questions, now is the time to be brutally honest with yourself and Her, because very soon there'll be no time to discuss such things, and there probably won't be for another 18 years.

c) How She became pregnant?

If you planned it together, then you most likely feel joy, pride, relief, gratitude and a tremendously deep love for your wife or partner. If it comes as a bit of a surprise, then you might well feel all of these emotions if you are in a stable relationship, but equally it might also be an unwelcome shock if the timing or circumstances of her pregnancy or your partnership don't conform to your ideas of what they should have been. Were you there at the conception? Were you planning to stay together for the next 18 years or more, or does nine months feel like too big a commitment? In any of these cases (and even if it's a happy surprise) you are probably experiencing some degree of psychological trauma, fear, and a certain degree of ambivalence about the whole affair. Go to the pub and mull it over before you launch World War 3.

d) The state of your finances (and hers)

Can you afford it? For a short time at least, you are going to be the only bread-winner and your costs will soon start to increase exponentially. If things are tight now then undoubtedly you are going to be worried about how you are going to be able to afford a new baby and all the paraphernalia that they need. Just make a mental note for the future that you are going to need money for:

Baby Kit (car seats, pram / buggy, playpen, high-chair)
Baby Clothes – multiples in ever growing half-sizes
A reliable washing machine and tumble drier

Toys - in a growing mound of age-appropriate brightly coloured plastic
Food – or something that almost looks like food initially anyway
Babysitters, childcare, au pair, nursery, pre-school
A bigger house, a bigger car, and life insurance.
And you won't have so much spare time - so overtime is not an answer. Start
saving NOW.

Exercise 1:

Profit & Loss Presentation to the Board

Your first exercise is to make a credible presentation of your personal Profit & Loss analysis to the Chairman of the Board.

Part One: Profits
Two weeks of paternity leave
Understanding why your Dad went grey
Another really important woman in your life (your daughter), or
A lifelong pal to take to football matches and the pub (your son)
The particular interest of Social Services in your personal life and finances
The opportunity to spend hours in supermarkets spotting Yummy Mummies
A grudging acceptance by your Mother in Law that there is ONE thing you can do well

Part Two: Losses
Any form of spontaneous "loving relationship" with your wife or partner
The freedom to do what you want, whenever you want
A totally carefree attitude towards your finances
The right to a sound night's SLEEP
Most of your single mates
Any form of privacy
SEX

Part Three: Presentation
Now turn to your wife/partner and tell her it is all worthwhile, remember she's the one who's going to be carrying your child for the next few months. If, under interrogation, your losses list outweighs your profits list, lie convincingly or be prepared to sleep in the spare room for the next 18 years.

Scaling the Rock Face of Life

Before we start talking about your children, let's start by discussing your favourite subject: YOU. The first thing to do as a Dad is to put yourself into the right frame of mind for fatherhood. You may have believed that up until now you were the centre of the Universe and, despite all heartfelt statements of undying love for your current wife and/or partner, your journey from undiluted bachelor hedonism has really been very short. The advent of a new child is a milestone in your life, and indeed, is a life-changing event unlike any other. From now on, you will have to take responsibility for another human being who is totally reliant upon you for its welfare – and if you think for a second that this statement is only true for the first 18 years of its life then you have a real shock coming in 19 years time. This is undoubtedly a daunting prospect – and one that is going to make you grow up really quickly. Sorry, but that's life!

On the other hand of course, there have to be some benefits or else the human race would have died out long ago, and might not have progressed out of the primordial swamp in the first place.

"No one ever dies saying "I wish I'd spent more time in the Office."

Hang On! I haven't finished yet!

Apocryphally, deathbed 'daddy regrets' seem to express the wish that they'd played more with the children, or that they'd travelled more or that they'd told X, Y or Z that they'd loved them - normally a wife, but sometimes a College girlfriend and, occasionally, the aerobics instructor in the local Gym. All of these unfulfilled experiences are things that we always meant to do, but never did. It may be that we were too busy with tomorrow to think about today. But when we suddenly find, to our great surprise, that it's time to go we often find that we've left it too late to do the things that we'd "always meant to get round to" in the spare minute that never quite arrived. If you don't take anything else from this Handbook, then take this lesson: make sure that you don't end up on a fluffy escalator, hopefully heading for eternal bliss, with the nagging worry that the Celestial Gatekeeper is going to ask you some awkward questions.

"You are not perfect, nor are you ever likely to be."

Sorry to disillusion you but just accept the fact that you're human, you're doing the best you can and at least you got as far as reading this book. Even if you didn't buy this useful tome for yourself, and were given it *in absentia* at a Baby Shower or found it in your Christmas stocking, somebody thinks that you, your children and your marriage are worth saving . . . even if only to use as a Bad Example to the others.

"The ONLY thing stopping you from being a good Dad is YOU and your perception of what is important."

At this early point in the Course, your ideas of what is important to you probably differ greatly to ours. So, we have another short exercise for you to complete so that you can take stock of what you think is important and put it into priority order. A word of caution before we begin: do NOT do the initial part of this exercise in the company of your partner or her mother, unless you have a completed a last Will and Testament and wish to taste the Divine Wind rather earlier than you had otherwise planned. Save it until you have reviewed it again at the end of the chapter and earn yourself a metaphoric pat on the head and the opportunity to extend the paternal bloodline as she cuddles up to you in praise of your thoughtful selflessness.

Exercise 2

Relative Priorities

Look at the list below and place them in what you feel is their proper order of importance. Write down your list of priorities and put it safely on one side. Don't be tempted to 'look good'. If money is more important than fluffy kittens, then say so! If something isn't important then leave it out. And the order below is alphabetical......

1) An early, comfortable retirement	2) Eating out
3) Foreign holidays	4) A fulfilling job
5) A fulfilling life	6) A good car
7) A happy, fun-filled life	8) Health
9) Intellectual stimulation & cultural pursuits	10) A job with maximum income (for minimal time & effort)
11) Lots of holidays	12) Lots of kids
13) Lots of sex	14) Professional success
15) The respect of my friends	16) The respect of the community/company
17) Sport	18) Status
19) Time for me	20) Time for my family
21) Time for our friends	22) Time to 'do my bit'

As an interesting comparator, ask your wife/partner/impending Mum to fill in the same table independently.

Hint Number 1: do NOT show her your list and keep a very blank look on your face when you read her list – she'll be looking for any slight twitch or facial tic that might betray the fact that your list differed drastically from hers.
Hint Number 2: defensive mothers are the most dangerous form of any species on the planet.
Hint Number 3: get her to show you hers BEFORE you show her yours (Remember the playground game?)

The Rock Face of Life

There is a fundamental rule in rock climbing, called 'Three Points of Contact', which states that when attached to a rock face, a climber should always retain three points of contact in order to remain in a stable position. Most normal human beings use four natural points of contact (two hands, two feet) and the use of elbows, knees, tongue or anything else that sticks out is distinctly frowned upon. When moving from one position to another up the rock face, only one point of contact should be moved at any one point in time – moving two at a time can be done as a calculated risk, moving three is a definite NO-NO and moving four at a time is called Freefall. The same rule applies as we scrabble up the Rock Face of Life where we have a similar set of four natural points of contact, but this time they are made up of Home, Health, Work and Wealth.

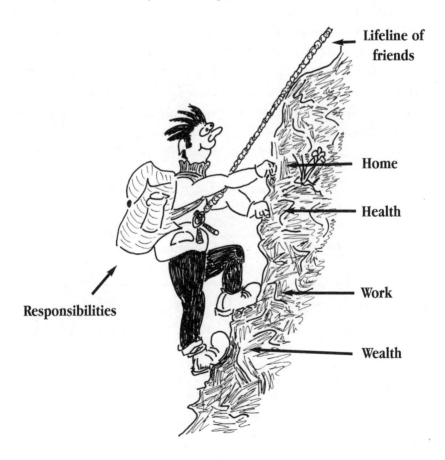

Lifeline of friends

Home

Health

Work

Wealth

Responsibilities

At the same time, each climber carries a rucksack filled with responsibilities (wife, children, mortgage, tax, bills, bills and more bills), which with the aid of gravity, is constantly threatening to pull him/her off the rock-face. You can survive if you follow the golden rule of climbing and retain three Points of Contact: if your health goes, due to serious illness for example, then you can still hang on so long as you've got good home support, a stable job and some money stashed away somewhere. Equally, if your home life falls apart, through divorce or death of a partner, then so long as you've still got your health, a job and some loot then you're still stable. Try out any permutation of the other combinations and you'll see that it still holds true. However, if you take off two or more hand-holds then you'll soon see how you become 'unstable'. With four 'Points of Contact' removed, you go over the edge and are likely to end up with a kerbside pillow and soup kitchen meals washed down with methylated spirits. Relatively few of us are 'free climbers', so there is another safety feature - in the form of a line that can be tied to the climber. This is provided by other climbers perched on the same rock-face who provide a safety line that is able to take the strain when one or more of your handholds comes unstuck. The more true friends you make as you climb, the stronger the bonds will be and thus, the stronger the safety line. If we take a look at our handholds a little further, we can see that they also have a definite priority order which parallels Maslow's classical Hierarchy of Needs.

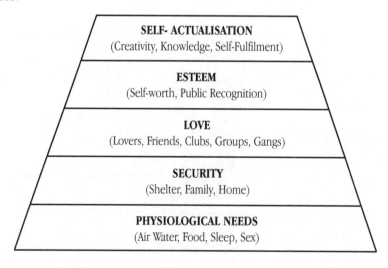

SELF- ACTUALISATION
(Creativity, Knowledge, Self-Fulfilment)

ESTEEM
(Self-worth, Public Recognition)

LOVE
(Lovers, Friends, Clubs, Groups, Gangs)

SECURITY
(Shelter, Family, Home)

PHYSIOLOGICAL NEEDS
(Air Water, Food, Sleep, Sex)

Without breaking our earlier promise of no psychobabble, and by way of a brief explanation, the theory of the hierarchy of needs states that human beings are motivated by unsatisfied needs, and that certain lower needs need to be satisfied before higher needs can be met.

Targeting your Life

In our analogy, the first and foremost requirement is Health, because without it you can do very little else. You owe it to yourself and your family to keep yourself in decent nick: playing football or touch rugby with Leg Limpets or 'tweenies can get pretty exhausting when they have a bottomless pit of energy and you only have an extra 10 pounds around the midriff. It only gets worse as you get older and your Gangly Lions start to test themselves physically against you. Second priority goes to Home because it provides you with the stable base from which to operate and a secure position to take physical and emotional cover when the rest of the Universe seemingly hates you. Home is also truly where the heart is and if your focus is maintained on creating and building family ties and structures then you will find it pays dividends later in the child-rearing process. Thirdly comes Work, because, for most of us men, it provides the means to exercise our personal intellect, knowledge, ambitions, creativity and, hopefully, to create Wealth, the last of the four 'stabilisers'. Your Friendship Lifeline comes into play across all of these priority circles to help when any one of the handholds comes off the rock-face. In the final analysis, your truest friends will be there, even when you are in freefall, trying to keep you hanging on. You too have the same part to play for your friends, family and children – just remember it when they need you.

The problem comes when we get these priorities wrong – and it's so easy to do. The modern pursuit of the Big Boy's Toys game (he who dies with most toys wins), is utter bunkum for anybody who wants to be a good Dad. Focussing on wealth first only works if you are guaranteed good health, have no family to distract you and have a job that totally absorbs you. This normally happens only when you're a young, carefree, bachelor with good career prospects and all thoughts of Daddyhood are best retained by a thin wall of sensitised rubber. If ever you have had a serious illness or have held your seriously ill child you will

13

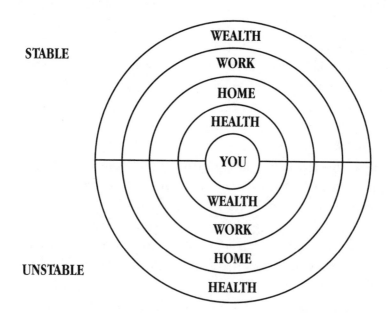

immediately understand how you would give up EVERYTHING in order to have these things back again. Let's go back to the last Exercise: assess your list again and see if you want to re-prioritise your order of things. If you still won't believe us then ask the lady who lies beside you in bed most often what she thinks - if it's your mother then you're too young to be reading this book, and if it's your mistress then reassess Handhold Number Two.

All things are replaceable, unless they cannot be bought

If you concentrate on your health, your time and the people for whom you care, the rest will fall into place. St Peter, or whoever you personally perceive your Heavenly Gatekeeper to be, is not going to ask you to list your possessions or ask for your bank statement on entry. The real game of life is NOT to see how many Big Boy's Toys you have when you get to the top of the mountain, but how many people from your Circle of Friends are waiting to say "Well done" when you get there. 'Champion of the Mountain' goes to the climber most truly loved, for how he climbed the rock-face and how he helped others up it too by pulling on their lifelines when needed. Unfortunately, few of us learn this early enough to affect the course of the climb and we remain scrabbling our way up adding extra loads into our rucksacks as we go.

Exercise 3

The Circle of Family and Friends

I. Take a pen and mark within the circles below how important things are to you, with the centre of the circle being of most important and the outer circles being less important. Make a separate mark for: your wife / partner, each of your children, your parents, your in-laws, your best friend, your close pals (name them), and your workmates. Some may be within the same ring, at different points of the compass.

2. Now consider the relative positions of those you have marked.

3. Ask your wife/partner and each of your children old enough to write to complete the same exercise on a separate sheet of paper using the same diagram.

The most interesting part of this exercise is the analysis and discussion of relative positions when you compare all the sheets together. Try not to cry when you find yourself on the outer edges of their sheets and question whether you should still be getting home deliveries when the milkman is on the inner circle.

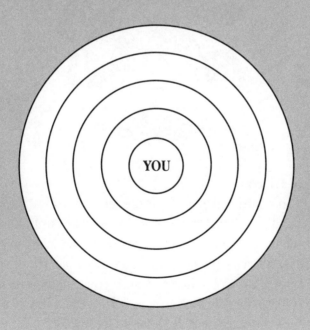

The Circle of Friends

It is worth noting that within the Circle of Friends those closest have ties that are strongest and more durable with support structures that are inextricably woven between them. These ties and support structures lessen in strength as the relationships weaken in progression towards the outer circles until, in the outer regions there are proportionally more Leeches - those who want more things from you than they are likely to give back in return. Beware the Land of the Unknown on the outer circle, for here are the Vultures: those who would devour your very carcass were you to fall in their company. If your offspring are to survive in the real world then it is up to you to ensure that they are aware of the Leeches and Vultures, can recognize them and shoo them away when necessary. It is also up to you to develop and strengthen the Circle of Friends, and to encourage your children to form and nurture their own circles of friends to provide the support structures that will see them, and you, safely past the Leeches and Vultures that will inevitably view them (and you) merely as another meal-ticket. Look closely at where you place your relatives and friends for it will show you which relationships you should work at to improve and, if you have tried to place markers in an unbiased fashion, where your perceived support structures lie. A word of caution though, when the excrement hits the extractor and real friends are needed, it is not always those whom you initially placed near the centre of your circle who stand fast when the tide of life turns against you. After such an experience, you might find that you need to redefine the circle.

Regurgitant

You may feel of course that this advice is vomit-worthily superfluous or mawkish as you sit in the comfort of your secure, suburban loo, set as it is in a generally peaceful, democratically governed, welfare state. But the problems caused by a mis-ordering of basic priorities are felt by children across the world, regardless of their economic, social or political background. Children just want their Dad's attention for a few minutes each day, or at best each week, and it doesn't matter whether you are playing with sticks in the dirt with them, or teaching them how to fly your latest helicopter. Indeed, many of the wealthiest people in the world spend so little time with their children that they hardly know them and then wonder why they turn out to be Micro-Monsters from the Planet Brat. Meanwhile some of the poorest families in the world are the strongest and most caring. If you get your priorities right then you, and your children, will end up having a much better quality of life and lasting relationship than if you'd just followed the Quest for the Holy Dollar. A collection of other sermons can be obtained from the "Daddy's College" School Shop along with some very natty stick-on wings for those Students who chose the right priorities in Exercise 2 without any coercion.

Homework:

During the next week, try reordering your lifestyle according to the following priorities:

Health

1. Ask your pregnant wife how she feels and if there is anything you can do to help. Make sure you mean it, because she'll spot an insincere question or offer. Remember, her body is currently in turmoil and anything you do in terms of back massages, carrying the shopping, or doing the washing will help lift the burden from her both physically and, more importantly, mentally.

2. Have a look at Men's Health magazine, which is one of the best publications for amusing you whilst also educating you about a healthy, active lifestyle. Try to concentrate more on the articles concerning healthy eating and exercise than propagation of your sex life – if you get the first two right the latter one will probably follow anyway.

3. Do something physically active for yourself each day and try to encourage each member of the family to do something for themselves as well (Bonus Mark if you manage to do it together). Getting up to find the TV remote control or fluffing the sofa cushions do NOT count.

Home

1. Spend at least one hour in the company of your partner with no other distractions (No TV/Radio, children, books, friends etc)

2. Spend at least 30 minutes playing with each of your children. If you are a brand new Dad, spend at least 30 minutes trying NOT to play with your new baby, just hold him/her and give the new Mum half an hour's break.

Work

1. Make sure that your boss and workmates know your happy news. Not only will they want to buy you a beer, but they'll understand if you need time to attend the hospital for pre-natal checks and help carry the load when the big birthing day comes. Most importantly, discuss with your boss how much time you are going to need as paternity leave to support your wife (and possibly look after your other children) when the baby is due.

2. Get home to see the children for at least an hour BEFORE they go to bed. (Bonus mark if YOU read them a story of their choice)

3. Take your child to work so that they can 'see' where you go and what you do. (If you happen to be the Bomb Disposal Officer for the Metropolitan Police, invent a cover job

18

to keep them amused. If you happen to work in MI5 , take them anyway – they'll never believe it and the Department will just treat them as new recruits.)

Wealth

1. Get a big jar and put your children's names on it. Place it where you come in from work. Every weekday put your 'shrapnel' into it.

2. Open a savings account for each child and make an occasion of going to make a deposit together.

3. Pick a children's charity to support and put your name down for a sponsored run/climb/walk/paddle/jump – anything whilst you have the last vestiges of energy and spare time!

"Darling, we're pregnant!"

Educating Daddy

2
Happy Birthday to You
Preparation for the big day

How to help with morning sickness, backache and food fads

Months 1-3

It's All New: the hormones, morning sickness, severe nausea at the sight and smell of certain things - now think what SHE is going through! It's all different and SHE will be getting very tired very easily. There's not much you can do about it or to help – except to provide comfort and a sympathetic sense of humour. Pick your jokes very carefully. Remember that the reward for supporting her is going to be that SHE gets to drive back from every party over the next nine months because alcohol is not very good for pregnant mums. Do not be too smug about it though, SHE will not let you forget for the following nine years.

Months 4-6

This is usually Glow and Show Time, though some less fortunate mothers may have a nightmare pregnancy and may feel rotten, or worse, for the whole nine months. SHE should feel much better and will become more attractive by the day (the Glow). Don't worry it's just the hormones and Mother Nature's way of apologising for what she is about to do to her body. SHE can still ski, ride, bonk and play tennis – do it while you both still can. Towards the end of this period, or trimester for the scientifically pedantic, SHE will start to show and the Bump will start to become more active as it begins to stretch, back-flip, kick and perform low-impact aerobics. You will start to take an almost unnatural interest in babies: you will notice them all around you, where once they were almost invisible; you will stop off at the parenting shelves in the bookstores and you will even start to believe that your Bump can hear you talk and that it will recognise and respond to your voice. You could try playing music to it: Mozart for the academically gifted, ZZ Top for the more mechanically minded or P Diddy if you want a snazzy, rappin', cool dude Mini-Me.

Months 7-9

SHE is now Bored By It All and you are going to become rather useful to her as a masseur and Gopher (Go fer this , go fer that). Massage will be demanded, especially for her lower back which takes the strain of the extra weight inside her, and foot massages will be requested to relieve the weight on her feet; these can be a rather good precursor…… Your greatest help will be as psychotherapist to relieve her anxiety. Remember that neither of you have done this before and it's a bit like parachuting: the bags are packed, she's standing in the door waiting for the green light and once she's jumped there's no going back. Your job is to make sure that she lands gently.

"SHE can give birth on her own, but SHE shouldn't have to."

a) Get Involved

She will appreciate all of your support especially if you take a real interest and help with the setting up of the Baby's Room, buying the vast array of new things you're going to need and if you attend the pre-natal classes with her. It will be amazing when you go for the ultrasound scans, but don't ask them to scan *your* abdomen and try not to bore too many of your workmates and relations with the cloudy photos of the Bump for too long afterwards. While playing 'Spot the Willy' is a really good game you should be careful if you are then going to decorate the spare room, line up the colour-co-ordinated outfits and choose names accordingly – you might not have seen what you thought you saw. Taking an interest can be fun and absorbing and is a natural and effective way of tackling the early-learning part of being a good Dad. So don't think that you're looking really soppy or stupid doing it – most other Dads have been through it and smile in gentle understanding whilst your still-single, guffawing mates just haven't woken up to what will come their way one day.

b) Pack Your Bags

SHE'll do her bit but remember that babies don't know what time of day or night they are booked for and there can be some delay in arriving. So you might also need a bag, or small backpack for swift movement through the hospital corridors, containing:

- A good watch for timing contractions.
- Pen and paper / Post-Its.
- An iPod, Walkman, or portable CD player and headphones.
- An acceptable book or magazine (leave the Playboy under the bed).
- Change for the vending machines and hospital telephones. Remember that mobile phones cannot be used in most hospitals since they can affect the monitoring equipment etc.
- A list of contact numbers for anxiously awaiting family and friends.
- A change of clothes? It can get messy or you might be there for some time.
- Food (but make sure it doesn't go rotten in the bag if you pack it two weeks in advance).
- Drink – for during the 'Waiting Game' and a bottle of bubbly for post-delivery celebration.

The Birth Day

Despite what the doctors say, the baby did not get the original briefing about normally taking 40 weeks to think about being born. It may well decide to come early or hang around in its nice, warm, comfortable womb. You may find that a hot curry, a hot bath and an amusing tumble between the sheets may help it on its way around D Day, and don't worry that Excalibur is going to hurt the baby: no matter what you may have boasted to the lads down at the Sports Club, it ain't that big.

"Your baby will decide when – but it won't book an appointment."

Whenever the Bump does decide to come it will be a bit of a surprise. You have a vital role to play on the big day: Taxi Driver and Chief Supporter, so do try to make sure you're sober around the due date. Time the contractions; get the bag in the car and make sure that you have a print out of the Birth Plan, so that it's all clear and plain when SHE asks for an epidural and you ask for nitrous oxide. Rehearse the breathing, play relaxing music; comfort, soothe, massage and, in the immortal words of the Hitch-Hiker's Guide to the Universe: "DON'T PANIC!"

Are you going to be there or not? Well that's for you and your wife/partner to decide, but you might think about getting a standby Birthing Partner, Justin Case, so that if you cannot make it home in time, SHE isn't left on her own. Waterloo was just as bloody, just as noisy and just as euphoric if you were one of the ones still standing when it was all over. If you do decide to be there, SHE will appreciate the company, you'll get to see it all, and a bit more, and you might get the chance to ask the midwife to slip in a couple more rows of catgut for good luck while she's practising her loop stitches round your darling's nether regions. On the other hand, and about 15% of Dads do, you might feel too uncomfortable, scared of being a spare prune or just too squeamish for such a quasi-religious experience, in which case you can pace around the waiting room worrying like your father did, though you'll have to promise to make up for it over each and every one of the next 18 years.

Exercise 4

A two part simulation of pregnancy and childbirth

1. Visit your local MegaBowl and borrow a size 16 bowling ball. Load it into the front of your T shirt and knot the lower end so that it can be carried as if it were a baby. Walk around MegaBowl for 3 months.

Cautionary Note: If you leave MegaBowl with the bowling ball under your T shirt, be sure to explain to the Manager that you are simulating pregnancy not practising a peculiar form of sports-oriented kleptomania.

2. When you have finished helping the Police with their enquiries about the unfortunate incident at MegaBowl, take Exhibit A (a size 16 Bowling Ball) and insert it into your Y-Fronts. Take a length of baling twine which is two inches shorter than your inside leg measurement. Attach one end to the Bowling ball and loop the other around the Family Jewels. Allow the Bowling Ball to fall on your toes. Repeat on alternate feet at gradually increasing rates over the next 3 - 12 hour period. Breathe deeply and smile if anybody asks you if you want gas or an epidural. Return Bowling Ball. The swollen ankles will help illustrate your case when you appear at the Magistrates' Court.

The point is that pregnancy and childbirth are impossible to simulate. But while you may not ever understand what your wife/partner is going through, you can empathise.

The Pain of Childbirth

There is one thing you can be sure of in this life: as a man, you will never have to experience the excruciating pain of giving birth. Be thankful for it and try to understand when, in the last stages of labour, SHE looks deep into your eyes as, with sweat pouring off her brow, SHE grips your hand in the tightest of vice-like grips that makes you gasp with wonder at her strength and you realise, wincingly, why SHE was filing her nails into stiletto-like talons just after her waters broke. Try not to cry and just concentrate on where SHE learned to swear like a trooper.

Paternity Leave

Make sure you give advance warning to your Boss and workmates. You *can* take time off and remember, NO MAN IS INDISPENSIBLE. Imagine life around you as a bucket of water, you only have a presence whilst your hand is immersed in the bucket and, though some ripples might remain as you extract it, there's little left once the waters close over the top. In reality, the best you can hope for is to leave a mark on the rim of the bucket. You can take time off, but plan it to

We think he's got his father's nose as well......

ensure that it is used most effectively: if SHE is going to be hospitalized, then stay in the office and save the days until SHE and the baby return home so that you can be of most use to both of them then. You can then phase in the home-help with both of the new grandmothers who will already have bought their Early-Bird Return Train tickets by the end of the first trimester.

Monkhood

Your domestic routine is about to change drastically and you will have to fit in with the new focus of everybody's attention which, surprisingly enough is

NOT YOU. It can be quite lonely, but….hey, it's new, you're not and you'll get your turn in about three months time, for about five minutes while you give the Proud Father's Speech at the Christening. It could be worse, if you'd been born a spider you'd already have been eaten to provide nutrients for your unborn young.

For now, you are going to have to endure your home-life going totally topsy-turvy as dinner, showering, TV, sleep, sport (don't even think about sex) and even work are going to have to fit in with the baby's timetable for feeding, excreting and sleeping. He/she or it is totally dependent upon you and the new Mummy for everything and whilst you perhaps have the chance of personal gratification, one way or another, he/she or it doesn't. So, for the moment at least, YOU are definitely in second place, if not third or fourth behind the dog and the goldfish. Just remember to take care of yourself during this period, because nobody else will be interested really; get down the gym, eat and drink sensibly, give up smoking and try to snatch some sleep so that you can endure the months of disturbed slumber from late night Evensong and sparrow-fart Matins. Feel like a monk yet? You will.

Educating Daddy

3
After the birth
Bringing it all back home

Assuming that you're a new Mum and Dad, you'll probably have opted to have your baby in hospital, so that for the first few days you'll have been surrounded and supported by cool, calm, and collected professionals. You face the next stage without such support, in your own home, and there will be a host of potential problems to face and solve. You may have to face them while simultaneously coping with your own near-total exhaustion.

Feeling Down

"SHE cannot control her depression."

Now's the time to talk about Depression – both hers and yours: hers will occur naturally as part of the hormonal rebalancing and there's nothing strange, abnormal or weird about it. Imagine PMT with claws: savage mood swings, inexplicable crying, the heavy stress of responsibility, sleeplessness, exhaustion, lack of confidence, resentment. It sounds like 'Work' doesn't it? **BUT**, and that IS a strongly capitalised and emboldened 'but', there is little SHE can do about it and there is a lot that you can do to help her. The good news is that it generally hits at about Week 1 or 2, only lasts for a few days or a week and not every Mum gets it. So your part may be short-lived but it is definitely essential: take as much responsibility for the baby as possible, make sure that SHE gets as much rest as possible, help with the household chores (find the Hoover and spend a few minutes figuring out how it works), cook dinner (healthy food NOT a bachelor's Cholesterol Special), go for a walk with them both or look after the baby while she goes to see a friend and, most importantly, talk to her – and not just about the football.

Your depression will have nothing to do with newly released hormones and instead will have everything to do with increased testosterone levels from the re-absorption of unused seminal fluid and to the anxiety levels that increase in direct proportion to the decrease in available capital in your bank account.

Educating Daddy

Breast feeding and other Liquids and Solids

They are no longer yours. Mork and Mindy will come back to you in a few months time, but for the moment they have another mission that takes precedence over your desire for ear-warmers. Whether your baby is breastfed or not is not your decision. SHE will decide if she wants to follow the natural path or move swiftly on to formula feeds. Choose the path of least resistance and support her choice, it'll make both of your lives easier. You will get your turn on the bottle though and it's worth noting that you should:

• Test the temperature of the feed on the back of your hand first. If it's at all hot, rather than quite warm, then leave it to cool or run it under the cold tap. The resultant two hours (?) crying from a baby's burned tongue with two months lashing from a Mum's outraged tongue should be enough of a deterrent to stop your pre-emptive shove of the teat into the baby's mouth.

• Keep to the recommended measures. Like most men, you will hate reading all of the instructions. But this time, do it and keep to it or else you will cock up the mixture and the baby will either end up with goo or misty water. Either way you'll pay for it at the other end.

• Feed the baby as though you had boobs. Hold it where it's Mum would hold it if she were breastfeeding it, let it look at your ugly mug whilst it's noshing. Try to imagine what it's thinking whilst it's looking up at you. Try not to go all gooey, it just thinks you're ugly and stupid really.

The move onto solid foods will occur from about the sixth month mark. After nappies, it is probably the most horribly messy experience you will encounter in the next few years. Babies have no sense of propriety or tidiness and, in fact, delight in the wonderful patterns that food can make over any surface. Indeed, a dissertation on "The splash effects of semi-soluble solids on natural and man-made fibres" is likely to be a sure-fire winner for any infantile undergraduate of Domestic Terrorism. Just be careful when they go on to study their Masters Degree with a paper on "The Causes of Catastrophic Failure in Ribena-filled

30

TimmyToppee beakers (supported by ballistic measurement and projectile experimentation)". Wear a bib and old clothes if you approach the Danger Area. Be prepared to adopt the role of Daddy Dustbin where you will find the left-overs quite enjoyable so long as you shut your eyes and just work on the taste not the view of the goo.

Interpreting cries and illnesses

You are about to find that you have gained a seventh sense that galvanises you and Mum like no other– it is the sound of your new baby crying. Interpreting each cry is a novel game that, like the baby itself, is easily picked up. Your baby will only cry when it needs something and at this stage its needs are relatively straightforward, give it a few more years and you'll be desperately wishing it was still so simple. The main causes of crying are, in baby priority order: hunger, discomfort or pain (normally nappy oriented, but possibly too hot/cold or windy), too tired to sleep, bored or lonely, scared and frustrated or angry. All you have to do is work out which reason it is and do something about it. Sounds easy doesn't it? Just wait.

Actually, don't wait. You'll find that if you react quickly, your baby will cry less and for shorter periods than if it is used to having to shout out for attention.

Babies live in the Here and Now and that next bottle, wet nappy or windy tummy will occupy 100% of its attention until you do something about it. The corollary is that you will not be able to concentrate on anything else properly until you have done something about it, so just get on with it as soon as possible and all three of you will be happy.

> *"Babies don't cry for no reason,*
> *you just need to find the reason, and then do something about it."*

The Crying Game

There are times though, when no matter what you do, your darling baby transforms into her demon child who just will not stop crying no matter what you try. You may find it helpful to try some of the following strategies which, curiously enough, seem to follow the prioritised list of causes for crying outlined earlier:

1) Feed the baby

No matter if it's not time for its scheduled feed, your child cannot read watches yet; don't be so anally retentive – your baby won't be!

2) Check its nappy

Imagine sitting at your desk with soggy pants. Could you concentrate on the CEO's 5 year strategy for corporate expansion? Check for humidity, smells, extra presences and rashes. Change nappy and add cream/powder as necessary.

3) Burp the little Herbert

If you go straight to bed after a big meal and don't move about to help the wind go up or down, then you'll get tummy ache as well. Picking up the baby and rubbing its back helps push out the air bubbles that form whilst it's sucking down its feed. Prepare for the inevitable posset down the back by chucking a cloth or towel over your shoulder first.

4) Rock it

Babies like a rocking motion and a 'shushing' sound which reminds them of the womb. If you haven't got a rocking chair, then try doing some half sit-ups with the baby held in your arms or across your chest – not only will it help distract you from the crying, it will also help restore your fitness and raise your serotonin levels. See who stops first.

5) Take it for a drive

Remarkably, babies like listening to Terry Wogan at any time of the day or night, especially if it's over the car stereo at 2 am as they gently cruise the neighbourhood in their babyseat or car-cot while Daddy desperately tries not to fall asleep. Make sure you're not likely to do so, and don't stop to ask that young lady with the very short skirt by the lamp-post if she knows where the best late night refreshment stand is located.

6) Wrap it up

It's a traditional method that makes your baby feel warm and secure– remember the Baby in the Manger – swaddling cloths?

7) Play with it

Amazingly enough, babies can be easily distracted by a highly colourful or soft toy......so can you, O Deliverer of Genes, remember the Porsche and the Blonde?

8) Give it to someone else

When all else fails and your patience is wearing really thin, take a break. Sometimes, even though you have tried everything your baby just will NOT stop crying. Keep calm, hand the baby to your wife / partner or any other trusted person and walk away – even if it's only for a few minutes.... she'll do the same to you one day, it's called partnership and it's essential in making sure that everything stays in perspective. You will be amazed, and perhaps a little disappointed, when the baby stops crying as soon as you've handed it over. Remember it is a heartless extortionist and it's just been trying out a new barbaric psychological torture on you.

Sleeping and getting into a routine

Standard Question: "Did you sleep well?" Standard Answer: "I slept like a baby." Conclusion: Your respondent slept for a bit, woke, cried, farted uncontrollably, went back to sleep for an hour or two, woke, wondered where everybody else was, cried again, slept for a bit, woke, wet himself/herself, wondered what to do about it and then decided to get everybody else in the house up as well. Whilst you may not invite such houseguests back again, you do not get the luxury of such an option with your own children.

Do not underestimate the effect that a newborn baby is about to have on you and your wife/partner's sleep pattern. Sleep deprivation is a well known and widely condemned interrogation technique used to break down an individual's ability to resist, to disorientate their sense of time, place and personal worth and reduce their ability to perform even the simplest of tasks properly. Whilst its use is specifically debarred under the Geneva Convention, most barbaric regimes still practice it along with other forms of brutal physical torture. Note that your baby is not a signatory to the Geneva Convention and, whilst currently incapable of giving you a direct physical beating, he/she will have no compunction in relentlessly depriving you of sleep in order to lower your ability to resist its demands. Think of he/she/it as a heartless extortionist interested only in extracting as much loot from you as possible before doing a runner leaving you with all the poo to clear up.

New babies do not sleep for long, their tummies are too small to take too much food at once and therefore they need to be replenished with small amounts fairly frequently. Parents therefore need to be on hand as required, which will be at regular intervals throughout the day and night. The only way to cope is to share the burden. Once SHE has finished breast feeding, or if she has 'expressed' milk into a bottle, let her go to bed early and let you as the Dad do the late night feed; SHE can then do the early, early morning and you can do the Sparrowfart Feed. That way both of you get at least some sleep so that you retain some form of sanity. Your workmates will notice your red eyes and habit of falling asleep in meetings. If they don't, then worry that you have been doing it for some time before you had a newborn baby in the house. Most importantly, note that whilst you can sleep in the office, your wife can't because the heartless extortionist has a 4 hourly timetable of demands that have to be met.

It is best to try to get your baby / infant into a regular sleep pattern as soon as possible. Remember that you are setting the foundations for your peace of mind and body for the next two decades: children love routine, since it reinforces their sense of security, and a bedtime ritual is a great way of establishing a sense of order and timing in the house. Besides, it then gives you and your wife/partner time to sit down and become real human beings with a real relationship again, rather than just knackered Mummies and Daddies.

Homework

1. Refer to your social diary for the 3 month period after the Due Date for the birth of your baby. Cancel all planned golf, skiing, rugby, trekking trips along with all other 'Boys' Trips Away'. Admit to yourself that SHE is pregnant, not just overeating lately, and your policy of self-denial is probably not going to work. Cry, and then get on with your life together, SHE is going to need your support.

2. In order to aid you through the first few months speak to as many other young Dads as possible to find out what they did, what shortcuts they found and what 'Poo Traps' to avoid. To make it both relaxing and useful for them and you, make the discussion venue in a pub: they'll need the opportunity to get out for a beer and you'll need to remind yourself that there are still lots of things in life other than new babies.

3. Do the same again, but make sure that both of you take your partners so that SHE can pick up some helpful hints as well and have her 'unspoken' fears calmed by someone who's "been there, done that, got the T Shirt with food stains on it". His comments on 'what Dads should do' will also be seriously vetted by his own partner for validity and as a positive help to you.

Health warning: You will encounter at least one smug new Dad whose offspring has never cried, and slept right through from Day 1. His time for more difficult days will come.

Educating Daddy

4
It Takes Two to Tango

"He moved his hands all over her body, as if to kindle each little part of it with his touch. Stroking her again from shoulders to thighs, he slipped his hands lower to reach the warmth within. With his kisses her hair had become more dishevelled, the dress has fallen off her shoulders and partly uncovered her heaving breast. She pulled him down towards the bed and started unbuckling his belt to release him from the confines of his. ..."

Ah, yes. You remember it so well: that sudden passion that swelled to a torrent of unbridled love, mingled with bodice-ripping lust. The Gods chortled in the knowledge that one of your genetic minions was about to win Gold Medal in the Ovarian Freestyle, because you couldn't stop to put on your swimming cap and she had already decided to increase Generation XL anyway.

Whose Responsibility ?

It's no good blaming her though, you did your bit, albeit for only about two minutes and 50 seconds according to the latest poll, and now you're going to have to face up to the responsibilities that go with the ever-swelling bulge of humanity that nestles within her. It takes two to tango, and making babies is the easy bit:

"Becoming a Dad is not hard, but being a Dad can be."

And therein lies the rub – you have to participate throughout the whole game, not just for the warm-up. It took two of you to make them - it also takes two of you to bring them up. This may sound glib, but it's amazing how many new Dads think that looking after the children is HER job, whilst quietly forgetting it's HIS job too. SHE just happens to be there for most of the day to allow you to escape to a more peaceful environment for about eight hours so that at least one of you has some semblance of sanity at the end of the day. BUT, the deal is that you take on some of the burden when you come through the door at the end of the working day. So if you want to flop and read the newspaper, do it in the car or pub before you get home, because you are in their time until the Little People are in bed and you've gently teased out what kind of day SHE has had. Getting frustrated when a Little Person is beating the back of your broadsheet is only going to increase your blood pressure, disappoint your progeny and alienate your partner. You would do better to negotiate a timeshare deal, where you devote 15 – 20 minutes 'quality time' to satisfy their immediate needs in return for an equivalent amount of Dad's Own time. Little People and Mums often understand and accept this time-swap and you'll end up with a completed cryptic and no cross words. Accept the fact that you cannot have your own life anymore – the rights you surrendered when you got married were nothing in comparison to those demanded from you in fatherhood – your life now belongs to them. This is a very important lesson for new Dads, so do yourself a favour and learn it early on.

Exercise 5

Division of Responsibilities

In every effective organisation there has to be a fair division of labour and responsibilities for it to function properly. Families are no exception and though the responsibilities are shared they are exercised in different ways through the roles of Mum and Dad.

Use the table below to work out who currently does what in your family. This time check it out with your wife / partner (Hint: we've filled it in for you)

Primary Responsibility	MUM	DAD	SHARED
Bed Times	X		
Clothes	X		
Drink (incl Alcohol)	X (Finds Out)	X (Deals With)	X (Worries)
Drugs	X	X	X
Food	X		
Getting into Trouble	X (Minor)	X (Major)	X
Homework/School	X		X
Luxury Items		X	
Money (Big Items)		X	
Pocket Money	X (Negotiator)	X (Banker)	
Playing/Playtime	X (Indoor)	X (Outdoor)	
Going Out	X (Organiser)	X (Banker)	
Sex Instruction	X (Girls)	X (Boys)	
TV/Playstation	X		
Tidying Up	X		

A post-exercise discussion will be highly illuminating to both you and her on current practical divisions of labour and potential future divisions. If you have older children, then it is also useful to ask their perceptions of which parent they regard as the ultimate authority on each area.

Health Note: Do NOT argue the toss when it comes to discussing the insertion of extra Xs into the Dad column above. Just go with the flow.

Footnote: Have a good Lawyer or Arbitration Service on call whilst sorting this list

The difference between a Dad and a Mum

A Daddy's Roles and Responsibilities

As a Dad your roles are as: PROTECTOR, PROVIDER, LAWMAKER and TEACHER.

As a Dad your responsibilities are to: PROTECT, PROVIDE, EDUCATE and SOCIALISE.

As Dads, you are primarily responsible for the overall needs of your whole family (that well-known rock group: Mummy and the Little People) in each of these areas. Mums tend to be primarily responsible for the daily needs of the Little People as the full-time carer, making sure that they are clean, clothed, cuddled, fed, watered, schooled, and behaving. They will look to you for ultimate authority and discipline, protection, to pay for everything and to be a source of Fun. It's down to formal negotiation between you and SHE to decide where the exact dividing line is drawn and, for the most part, you'll learn it on route but **the most important lesson is to agree and support each other during the journey**. Little People need to be told where the boundaries are and be brought back inside them when necessary. But they are also great at

Daddy's College Badge and Motto

QUOD SUM PATER
ET ITA DICO

Our next Blinding Glimpses of the Obvious comes from the ancient Coat of Arms for Daddy's College:

The Castle represents the secure and stable seat of protection; the Lion (Rampant, Guardant) represents Kingship, the ruler and law-maker of the family; the Sun represents the provision of life, light, warmth and energy – the means to make things grow; the and the Owl represents wisdom and knowledge.

The Motto means "Because I am the Daddy and I say so" and should be quoted frequently.

playing both ends against the middle – if you let them. Whatever happens, don't get drawn into the invidious position of letting them do something when SHE has already told them not to do so. Protect your own back, first and foremost by enquiring 'Have you asked Mum?' If they have then, go with the flow; if they haven't, send them back to First Base and if they lie, you're in the clear and they're dead meat. Whatever you do though, don't countermand the SHE decision until you've consulted the Oracle herself, or else you will lay yourself wide open to accusations of undermining her and giving them the opportunity to play you off against each other. The secret to a quiet life is Communication – ask her how SHE wants to play it or tell her what you've already decided and let her countermand you – whatever you do , don't let the Little People see any chink of weakness or they'll be through it faster than you can say "Because your Mother said so."

All disagreements with the above gross generalisations may be made to the Complaints Desk in the College Sanatorium who will be most grateful for the additional paper. Please ensur that you correspond on soft absorbent tissue only.

Three Ages of Childhood

In most traditional tribal societies, young boys are treated in three groupings, a kind of 'Three Ages of Childhood': from birth to about seven years old they reside in the 'house' of their Mother; from seven to 14 they reside in the 'house' of their Father and from 14 – Manhood they go to the 'house' of a Mentor or Guide. For young girls the process is similar except that when they hit puberty and potential sexual potency they are removed to a more 'protective' environment (see the section on shotguns and a Dad's Rules for Dating Daughters). Whilst the really Little People, **Leg Limpets**, will love to have you there and playing with them, when the chips are down it's Mum that they want. Our **'tweenies**, who live in that zone between infancy and teenagers, begin to need more active participation on a mental as well as physical level, and this is where they start to learn sports, hobbies and wider social interaction – largely based on the environment and examples they see around them. At this stage they will 'flip-flop' between being adorable angels and abominable monsters in a schizophrenic instant that is incredible to behold. The two closest and most trusted examples they have are their parents. How you behave in relation to them, towards each other, towards your friends, and the wider world will influence them more than anything else around.

Gangly Lions, or teenagers as they are more widely known, think that they are about to enter the Teenage Tunnel with only their hormones to guide them since you know nothing, understand nothing and have little worth other than as a taxi-driver and/or as a bottomless pit of funding. At this stage, your Little People are uncomfortably large, take up far too much of the settee for far too long and hoover up the contents of the refrigerator in an ever-constant grazing pattern more reminiscent of herds of migrating wildebeest. If your Gangly Lions turn into 'Ganglions' by hanging around for too long, becoming unsightly and embarrassing in public, then try the traditional remedy of hitting them with a weighty family bible or have them surgically removed. However, remember they are all Limpets, be it Leg-Limpet, Time-Limpet or Wallet-Limpet and you and their Mum are the rocks they cling to until the waves of Time wash them free.

Setting an example – your leadership role

Unless of course your children have left home already and you are checking out this tome as a Grandparent in order to castigate us as buffoons or to pass it on as a bible to your imbecile of a son/son-in-law so that he can have half a chance at getting Dadhood right, what matters most is that you recognize that your Little People are watching you all the time and that the magnificent little computers stacked behind the sticky jaws and cherubic smiles are logging your every move. Spooky huh? They are shaping themselves on you and their Mum, and your mannerisms, vocabulary and treatment of others WILL be mirrored through their own world. The next time you are in a supermarket, watch how different parents treat their own children; if you see a Mum shouting and swearing at a brace of snotty nosed, Marmite-coated tykes you can bet your bottom dollar that they'll grow up to do the same to their children. If that's how you want them to turn out, then fine and dandy, but if not then let's start looking at who they are going to use as role-models and what we can do about it.

"You are the most important influence in your children's lives."

Your Little People live in a smaller and slower universe than you do. They will look to you to set appropriate limits in what they can and cannot do, and notice very clearly if you do not keep to them yourself. They have an innate sense of fairness that is either reinforced or degraded by you according to how they observe both your behaviour and what you let them get away with. If you let

Children do as children see

them know it's OK to abuse, bully, cheat, and lie their way through the immoral alphabet, then that's what they'll do as they grow. The inevitable result will be a future member of an anarchic society with no respect for anybody or anything. As a Dad, you thus have the power to shape the future of the human race – an interesting thought eh?

Manners

There's an old adage that Manners Maketh the Man, so make sure that you teach them to do what you want them to do, in terms of etiquette, when you're not around.

"If you don't care about their manners, then they won't either".

If you have the table manners of Henry VIII, or if you insist on showing your gratitude for hospitality through expelling fetid air, then do not be surprised when the Little People follow in the path of their Hero. However, it's also a great feeling when someone you hardly know compliments you on the manners of your offspring – bask in the warmth of their words, secure in the knowledge that it is a reflection of the time, effort and training you've put into them. It might be old-fashioned, but part of a Dad 's job is to teach them how to respect other people and other people's property, how to address Big People properly until they are formally told to be informal, how not to interrupt, how to eat politely, and how to shake hands. For your sons, add on how to shave and how to knot a tie properly and, for your daughters, how to disable a man or boy within three seconds and how to make an Airborne-strength gin and tonic. In the ultra-modern world this extends to not taking or making a mobile phone call or texting whilst you're talking to somebody else – even if they are only a shop assistant or the dustman. Ingrain that into them.

Courtesy costs nothing but is highly valued. Despite their unfashionability, many of the old manners, like holding doors open or offering seats to ladies and the elderly, are still regarded as acts of gallantry and politeness and still seem to be truly appreciated by all but the politically correct champions of social and sexual egalitarianism.

The Immutable Laws of Daddyhood
Having sorted out the division of labour and responsibilities, there are still some fundamental laws of nature in this Universe, which, like gravity, death and taxation cannot be avoided. Just accept them and get on with your life.

As a Dad:
1) You cannot Multi-task – so don't try to do so
2) You NO LONGER get to keep the chequebook
3) You will NOT find the TV remote control where you left it
4) You will get disturbed just when the football/film is at its most crucial stage
5) Your children will love you, no matter how hard you try to ignore them
6) You will wonder where all the years went and how they got so big so quickly
7) Your teenage son will test himself out against you
8) You will never know what goes on in your teenage daughter's mind
9) You will always know what goes on in said daughter's boyfriend's mind
10) You will think it all worthwhile when you hold your first grandchild

Staying Involved
Getting involved starts from Day One and has nothing to do with being a

'Modern Dad' and everything to do with just being a Dad. In the first few years, getting involved is fun, novel and interesting; the harder thing to do is to ensure that you stay actively involved, despite the competing pressures of a progressive career, sport, DIY, the pub and anything else that you can use as an excuse to get out of the house. Your contribution over the next 18 or so years is going to be an invaluable one and you are no longer 50% of a couple but at least 45% of a team of three: for the mathematically minded, your percentage input per team member has increased NOT decreased and will continue to grow as you add in more junior team members.

In the early months, this consists of NOT pretending to be asleep when the early hours erupt with banshee shrieks from down the corridor. In the later years, you'll hear every floorboard squeak when there's a strange male in the house, so don't bother trying to con Mum that you sleep the Sleep of the Dead or by month two of your newfound Daddyhood, you might well be doing so. Since the new Little Person wants to sup at the onboard Milk-Bar during the early hours, try taking the late shift up to midnight and let the new Mummy get a couple of hours in early – she'll be a nicer person for it around breakfast time. Make friends with other Dads, and find out what they do. Forget the years of single-minded bachelorhood when you pitied married friends for their impenetrable shared conversations and crumpled photos of their children. You will find that, no matter how hard you try to resist it, you will be so proud of your new progeny that you will find yourself wanting to tell the world about this new discovery that you've made. Like-minded New Dads will inevitably be drawn to the same conversations. Pooled knowledge can be very useful and in the last resort you can go down the pub together.

"Skin is washable."

No matter how nasty those nappies smell, no matter how sick they've been and no matter how much your tummy churns at the thought, it still needs clearing up and they cannot do it for themselves. Everybody wees and everybody poohs. Expulsion of waste products is an inevitable result of the ingestion of oxygen, water and food and if you don't do it – you die. Everybody needs training on when to do it, where to do it and how to do it most hygienically – oh, and lots of understanding if they can't manage to pick these skills up quickly enough (according to your timetable). In HIS wisdom, the Great Engineer gave us all a warm, sensitive, regenerating, cling-film wrapper called skin. And here's the really great bit – it can be washed and reused again and again. So get stuck into those nappies lads, and learn how to do it properly so that you don't have to scrub all that skin off.

"Little People are really very resilient and tend to bounce back."

The human race has been around now for quite a few years with little real need for a design overhaul and, so long as you don't drop them on the end of the bonnet, most models will actually bounce quite well. We don't recommend that you try a practical lesson in this at all, just don't worry too much when you get your first bump/graze/rash etc. By the time your third child has one you'll be adopting a more spartan approach and wondering why it's crying as it hands you its left arm and asks whether you can stitch it back on before bedtime.

"Can you sew this back on, Daddy?"

However, one of the most important contributions you can make as a Dad is to learn early on about how to Control Temperatures. About a third of all under 5's have a Febrile Convulsion at some point - and you and SHE are going to panic when the first one happens to your child and you mistake it for the early signs of meningitis. (Go and look it up now and ease your mind – this is not, and is not intended to be, a medical journal and our insurance cover doesn't extend that far). If you haven't got a decent child's sickness reference book in the house – buy one tomorrow, or pick up one of the free pamphlets from your chemist and buy a First Aid Kit to go with it – you'll need them both before long.

Doing Your Fair Share – Parents NOT Slaves

It is also important to make sure that your offspring also know that your place in life, and that of their mother, is not that of domestic slave and that they too should get involved. Mary Poppins is a fictional character and, no matter how hard one tries, household chores just don't get done with a snappy click of the fingers. Equally, children will not naturally help around the house and need to be trained to get involved just as much as you do. If you want to succeed, you should start with jobs that are within their capability for their age.

For Leg Limpets, break down the list into simple tasks and give specific jobs that they can focus on like "make your bed, put your toys in the toybox and your books back on the shelf". You might have to give each instruction individually, only asking for toys to go into the toybox after the bed has been made. Children can be creatures of habit, and as such if you can incorporate little jobs into their routine (when they get up, they turn down the bed) and if they do any task unbidden, praise and reward them. The real secret is try to do things with them – and make it part of their and your playtime. You'll find it remarkably relaxing (re)discovering the joys of Playmobile and Lego.

And finally, remember that getting involved doesn't hurt. Your ego might be bruised because YOU are not centre stage anymore but the benefits really do outweigh the costs in the long term. Children might take up some of your time, they will take up some of your energy and they are certain to take up a lot of your money. But what else were you going to do with the rest of your life anyway?

Homework:

During the next week, Send your partner off to do something/see a friend (or even to visit the Wicked Witch of the North-in-Law). You look after the children for a whole day. If you have already crossed this hurdle then try a weekend of it and, if you're really adventurous or just truly masochistic, try a week of it.

List your mishaps (honestly) and list what you learned about the Little People and about how to look after them.

Caveats: No special treats, No crisps, Limit all E Numbers, TV watching restricted to 1 hour in the evening and Playstation to 15 minutes every other day. All homework/reading to be done. All to be in bed at proper time. No more than seven units of alcohol to be drunk in any 24-hour period (that includes Dads as well).

Guidelines: To be supplied by Mum before departure. (Food, activities, bedtimes, normal routine, Emergency Contact Numbers)

Disclaimer: Our Lawyers have asked us to insert a Special Disclaimer at this part of the Homework.

"All advice offered is on a goodwill basis and there is no compunction by any member of Daddy's College, Student or Staff, to believe, participate or follow any of the Course content. Indeed, any Mum who is daft enough to leave an untrained Dad in sole care of their Little People for longer than it takes her to go to the bathroom, is utterly barking and in need of full certification herself. Daddy's College and its Board of Education accept no responsibility whatsoever, for any accidents, mishaps or damage sustained by Dads during their education at the College or thereafter Amen."

Educating Daddy

5
Playtime

You have forgotten how to play, and you will forget how much fun it was within a day of every occasion that you do so.

***"Play with them when they ask you
because one day they won't ask you anymore, you'll be asking them."***

We are not talking about Big Boys Toys (the sports car, yacht, Play Station 3, etc), we're talking about real child's play with imaginary worlds, big monsters, multiple Doctor Evils, and Superheroes. Everybody is going to get shot and come back to life again, nobody gets hurt (unless it's scraped knees after falling out of a tree) and when the heroine (from next door) gives you an icky kiss you're going to go "Yeeucchh!" and hope it gets edited out of the script before your friends see it.

Having discussed roles and responsibilities in the last Chapter, you should be aware that Dads also have one additional important role that is fundamental to

The best toy in the world.

the Primary Years and takes on a wider aspect when you get to the Middle Ages and your child starts to develop interests and skills of their own.

"You are the best toy your child has ever been given."

You are renewable, rechargeable, immensely strong and flexible, and utterly unbreakable no matter how hard they try. What more could a Little Person want? Your sons will want to play Rough and Tumble as part of their boundary-seeking and bonding with each other and you – watch young lions or dolphins at play and they will display exactly the same characteristics in play as your youngsters do. You should also note the patience and care displayed by the flea-bitten old warrior lion as he lets the cubs buffet him in mock battle. Don't worry, he'll let them know when enough is enough –and so will you with your own imitable roar when it's time to settle down again. Your daughters will want to play a softer more ticklish version of Rough and Tumble, and will want to retreat quickly when it starts to get more Rough than Tumble – but, as the Dad, it's up to you to make sure that the boys recognize the difference and the limits early on.

Risk Management

Play is an important element of growing and learning. It's where Little People learn about social interaction and risk-taking. Of course you should care about what they are doing and with whom, but don't mollycoddle them or else they'll never learn to take a risk later in life. The current trend in the UK is to reduce children's opportunities to play outside for fear of a whole range of perceived dangers that did not appear to abound "when we were youngsters". If you think about your own childhood you will probably be struck by how much freedom you were allowed and, by comparison, how little you allow your own children. But perhaps we have become the victims of our own fears? Or perhaps it's our perception of risk that has changed and our kids are just as safe as they ever were?

Perhaps our children would be safer if we allowed more of them to play outside together and allowed UK society to become used to seeing children playing outside and taking more of a collective responsibility for ensuring that

Letting your children get some fresh air

they were safe? Removing our children from risk does not necessarily mean that we remove the risk from our children, it merely imposes a temporary local solution, whereas we should be looking for and implementing a longer lasting, general solution that is going to carry them through, and into, adult life. Risk to your children is not going to disappear, but, as in business, it can be recognized, managed and suitably mitigated so that they can grow and learn whilst still being protected as much as possible. The risk management of your family is your job – just make sure you agree a policy with their Mum.

The benefits of play (for a Dad)

It takes total absorption with a Little Person to remind you how to play properly. Try it and you'll see these things happen:

1. You'll note how much fun it is (for both of you).
2. How it de-stresses you without any real effort.
3. How much your Little Person loves it and wants more of it.
4. How much his/her Mum appreciates it.
5. How much you'll look back on it and get a gushy warm feeling that you'll never admit to in the bar of the Sports Club.

At home you can be sure that Mum will really appreciate the extra time and effort you take to play with the most important people in her life. Nobody else needs to know how much you really enjoy playing with ducks in the bath, nor do they need to know that Zondar, Monster of the Fifth Galactic Zone of Alpha Centauri, is also known as Mister Nigel Effinem, your Bank's Mortgage Account Manager, and that you took great joy in mangling his knackers with your Fantasmagoric Ray Beam when you were Marvello, Master of the Universe just before teatime.

"There's a Captain Marvello waiting to discuss mortgages..."

Rules of the Game

There are certain ground rules that Dads have got to recognize before they get involved in playing with their children, or anybody else's children for that matter:

1. You are there to play with them not vice versa.

Relax and enjoy the experience. Your role here is as their playmate and teacher, and it's your job to help them explore their world and their capabilities through an enjoyable number of play mechanisms. They can't play Tag or throw a ball on their own and you make a great partner to play with. Little People have wonderfully open minds that only need a little bit of prompting to kick into action and it's up to you to act as the sparkplug for their imagination-motors. In playing games, prompt them, show them how most people do it, but allow them the freedom to play it their way to begin with. They'll learn how to do it properly through experimentation and experience and, at the moment, they've got all the time in the world to practise.

2. Nurses and Patience.

At some point in your playtime together, you and they will get completely and utterly frustrated by their attempts to master an action or skill. You will nurse them through preliminary steps, but then you'll have to let them have a go for themselves and, seeing repeated failures and mounting frustration and temper, you'll desperately want to reach over and do it for them. Don't! Have patience and give them the time to practise it until they get it right. After all, would you get on their bicycle and ride it for them?

3. Player/Manager.

Whilst you have a role as a Player, you have a greater role as Manager and Coach. It might be difficult to do in the heat of the moment, but remember which one of you is the adult and which one is the child. Your job is to get the best out of your Star Player by supplying the knowledge, the means and constant encouragement. You also have other roles as Lab Technician, Product

Educating Daddy

Demonstrator, Librarian, and President of the Supporter's Club (with a lifelong subscription to attend each and every game). Just make sure you bone up on netball and hockey as well as rugby and cricket so that you know a bit about all of the games your players are likely to play. You may run in the Dad's Race on Sports Day, but do NOT take your trainers unless you feel happy being utterly derided in public and, if you do win, expect the delight of your 'tweenies and the horrified embarrassment of your Gangly Lions.

> *"When the one Great Scorer comes*
> *To mark against your name,*
> *He counts not that you won or lost*
> *But how you played the game."* [2]

This is a laudable epithet that should be instilled into every child from the earliest age despite its natural urges to win and despite the rather unpleasant modern trend to push our offspring to win at all costs. However, it is all very well just to urge them to take part and few of us are talented enough to be good enough to win all the time, but equally nobody likes to lose all the time either. Make sure that your child wins at least 50% of the games you play together – but

Engineer your own defeat – if you have to

don't get spotted throwing the game or you'll be accused of not playing properly. If necessary, handicap yourself so that you balance up the playing field: play with the wrong hand: give them a headstart in a race or some extra cards in the game. If necessary, invent an excuse or rule that allows them to make it more of a contest - that you could almost have won. Importantly though, you must demonstrate how to behave when you lose – and ensure that they do so when they lose too.

They won't play fairly if you don't play fairly. Little People have an innate sense of what's right and fair, which can be reinforced by you making them play by the rules. Of course you'll have to make some minor adjustments when they are little, but have a firm 'No Cheating' law and abide by it yourself. Remember, there is only one thing worse than being known as a Bad Sport or a Bad Loser and that's being known as a Cheat.

Exercise 6

Playtime for Dads

Dads of Leg limpets, should (re)discover the joys of playing in the bath. You will only need bubble bath, warm water and ducks/boats. Once tried, you'll fight Mum for the privilege next time. Ensure that your house insurance covers bathroom flooding first. Extend this game to the Swimming Pool, but don't take the bubble bath and ducks or everybody will want to play with them.

Play with me Daddy !

Listen to the lyrics of Jim Croce's song 'Cats in the Cradle' and you'll remind yourself of why you have to play with them when they ask you... one day the boot will be on the other foot and if it's not a habit with you now, how will they form the habit for later?

Toys and Games

The first few months of your child's toy-life will be filled with a profusion of cuddly soft toy replicas of cartoon characters and irresistible pink or blue rabbits, surrounding a cot above which is suspended an astrological mobile which incessantly plays Bach's Lullaby. Thereafter, Leg Limpets and Tweenies progress through a range of, hopefully, age-related toys that serve not only to develop their ability to pull, push, hit and throw, but also allow you to jump, dodge, step and roll as you find them littered around the house. Of course they can only really play with the toys that you give them, read the books that you borrow or buy for them and go to the places that you take them. You and Mum therefore, will determine what, how and where they play until they are old enough to decide for themselves. Make sure of course that their toys are appropriate to them or else you'll find them just getting frustrated or bored and yourself on a Mum-directed trip to the Early Learning Centre to buy something else more suitable. There is no need to buy new toys every week, even though the Far Eastern Plastic Fiend Companies would love us to do so, because you will find that the natural progression of Birthdays and Christmasses will accumulate an obscene mountain of mangled, brightly coloured, polysomething toys to clutter the darker regions of the garage. Old toys can easily be recycled through the use of a toy-box that is shuffled to re-introduce toys that had been long forgotten.

A Dressing Up box is a Must, and should be stuffed with old clothes, accessories and the contents of your Mother-in-Law's 1960s wardrobe. It will form a cheap but essential part of their Make Believe play, into which you will be invited occasionally, and which can keep them amused for hours on end. Surprisingly enough, a large card-box also often offers more enjoyment than the expensive item it contained and it's shelf-life as an amusement can be extended through the careful addition of a couple of portholes or flaps, some squiggly lines for waves and a broomstick. Sand and water are always good standbys, so long as you are careful to ensure that the water is fresh and the lid goes on the sandbox to prevent it from becoming a cat litter tray. Mum will probably introduce them to music through the medium of the Saucepan and Wooden Spoon Band, but you can also invent your own family games and rhymes with them. Try the "I Love You" Numbers Game, which Tweenies love for its silliness and Mums love for its essence. It alternates in escalating order between you and your Little Person as follows:

> "I love You."
> > "I love you Too."
> "I love you Three."
> > "I love you Four – Ever."

"I love you Three Million Four hundred Zillion and forty six (and a half)"
(Etcetera et cetera *ad infinitum* with giggles, cuddles and Mum's admiration).

Painting and Drawing

Little People love to draw and paint and seem to cover the breadth of artistic history as they develop. They progress from a splodgy, abstract load of Pollocks, through Lowry-like Matchstick-men and almost unnatural Impressionism, to reasonable resemblances of the world about them. Go with the flow of it, and urge them to experiment further – just not on the walls and doors of the house, unless you have a passion for interior decorating. But whatever you do, if you are unsure as to its form or favour, NEVER ask them what it is. They'll ask you if you can guess and your best escape clause is to offer a

"Well he may have no ear for music, Mrs Van Gogh, but he's always loved drawing and painting."

response so outrageous that they will automatically know that you haven't a clue. Accept the accusation of "Silly Daddy " and their delighted correction.

Card and Bored (sic) Games

Card and Board games can be a great way of 'doing things together' as a family, especially when the Great British Summer conspires to trap you all in the house for the day. Indoor games let your Little People practise their skills of counting and comparing numbers, shapes and colours along with making value judgements about what they should do next. They also allow for some deeper social 'Rules' to be learned so that the norms of 'taking turns', 'my go next', 'miss a go' penalties and 'no cheating' can be applied and practised in an entirely safe and controllable environment. Note the Rules of the Game above – especially those covering Winning and Losing: the intellectual effort required to plan and execute your own demise without getting spotted should more than compensate for your injured pride from the "Mummy, Mummy, I beat Daddy !" delighted whooping and crowing of a six year old. If they are still doing it when they are 16, then get a grip - you really aren't trying hard enough.

Television

Television is a wonderful thing that has brought much joy and spread much knowledge across the world but, as with all things in life, if not kept in moderation, it can be abused and can even take over one's life. The same logic applies to videos and DVDs. So it's up to you to set the rules over what you watch, how much you watch and when you watch it and, more importantly, it's

up to you and your wife / partner to agree a policy to determine for your children what, when and how much they watch. If you are firm then your offspring will accept your rules, but remember they have an Audiovisual Insatiability Motor which kicks in where television is concerned and will watch Constantly Repeated American Programmes (CRAP) *ad infinitum*, if you let them. There is a great danger that you unconsciously assign the role of Electronic Nursemaid to the television, because it's easier to bung the Little People in front of 'the Box' in order to allow you to get on with something else, than have to spend your spare free moments sitting on the floor with an alien playing with wooden blocks. The major problems created by the Electronic Nursemaid strategy is that your children develop poorer reading skills, are less physically active and get along less well with other children who watch less television and who are thus more socially adept. The dangers of television for your children are:

Too Much: An average of about two hours per day is about right to allow enough time to do something else. By the time, they've done their homework (a pre-requisite to the TV going on in the first place) done something 'outside' and had their tea, they'll be pushed to get in a two hour 'Glue-Time' anyway. TV in the morning, especially during term-time, fills their head with rubbish rather than preparing it for a day of accumulating useful knowledge: it's like having a blank sheet of paper and scribbling all over it before you write down your business plan. Try talking to them over the cornflakes about what they are going to do that day instead – you'll be amazed at the response.

Too Long: Little People need their sleep and even though television drops brain activity to neanderthal levels it is no substitute for a relaxing bedtime story, read by you or Mum, and a subsequent roomful of Zs. Excessive early morning grumpiness is directly proportional to excessive late night TV, it's the equivalent of the Little People's Hangover.

Too Strong: You should check out some of the other programmes that they watch regularly, since modern programmers seem to have their own views of what is socially acceptable, or else you will unconsciously abrogate your responsibility for what they watch to someone who has more allegiance to the sponsor than to you as a parent. We're all aware of the 9 o'clock watershed, but be careful of what you watch in front of the children if they are still up with you at that time of night. Most importantly, and in your role as 'the Dad', be actively critical of what they see on television, comment on it, especially on any bad language, bad social behaviour and excess violence and make sure they know why it is unacceptable. If you don't pull them up on it and make them critical about what they are observing then they will think that it is acceptable and will repeat it in the real world. Ensure they know that the most effective review for a bad programme begins with a "Click."

And Books

"If it's electronic you need to turn it on, if it's on paper you need to open it, but you will still need to be able to read it."

Boys' reading improves between the ages of 6 and 11 if their father reads to them: boys repeatedly lag behind girls in the national reading league tables and the percentage of boys who enjoy reading stories appears to have decreased from 70% to 50% over the past five years. Now, whether this is because there aren't sufficient books to interest boys or whether there is some gender -specific psychobabble that gives girls the edge, you can do your bit by reading to your little Herberts when you get the chance. If your work allows then 'book your slot' to read them their bedtime story, or set aside a specific period during the weekend to read to them, and to get them to read to you. A love of books is inherited and as natural as your reading to them should be. If your Little People grow up in a house where books are available, used and referred to often, then they will accept them as part of their everyday life. If they see you and your wife/partner reading then they will know that it is a 'normal' pastime and want to do so as well – as with any of the other areas of play – make reading part of the daily communal routine. There is an art to reading with a child: you will need material appropriate to their age and gender; you will need a quiet corner and the right amount of time so that no-one is distracted and you will need the imagination to retain their interest by involving them in the action. You'll also need the patience and stamina to take first place in the Leglimpet Marathon with the four hundredth reading of 'Flopsy Bunny's Fun-filled Frolics in Fairyland'.

Joining your local library is an excellent way of widening their interest in books by showing them the fantastic range that is available to them - for free. If you actually manage to take out a few books then you'll soon find that making a trip to the Library soon becomes a habit for them and you. And if books don't turn them on, as a last resort, buy them a comic – at least they're reading.

Fun for all the Family

If, like most Dads, you spend most of your week from Monday to Friday in the office or other workplace, then you will know how valuable weekends are to you and the rest of the family. Add to that the need for you to have some time to yourself to regain your sanity, and for your wife to have the same, plus the pressures of attending school/Club sports matches other activities and the time available to spend together as a family becomes very precious indeed.

Much of this family time will be spent in or around the home, so use communal activities to provide a forum for family interaction. Insist on eating together and make sure that everybody, regardless of size, gets a chance to tell the others what they've been doing and what interests them currently. If you have jobs to do around the house and garden, then recruit your Little People to help you. They love being involved as 'Daddy 's Little Helper', especially if you give them a special responsibility such as handing you the (non-powered) tools whilst you're hammering and screwing, or as 'Keeper of the Sponge' whilst cleaning the car. They might even push the wheelbarrow in exchange for a ride in it on the way back from the compost heap. If you have a particular sport or passion, then make sure that you involve them in it. Take them fishing with you with a small rod of their own; take them to Proms in the Park or to see your favourite rock group. You could give them the lifetime gift of 'a Team' to support and make sure that there is an 'arch-rival' team to castigate and lampoon. Children love having a 'Goody' and a 'Baddy', but make sure that they recognize the limits of good spectator support or else you'll end up raising your own football hooligans. It doesn't really matter what the activity is, so long as they are with you, doing something active and are being applauded for their assistance and company. Don't worry about the extra mess they make as they help you, it's a small price to pay for a major investment in the Bank of Fond Memories.

Family Outings and Treats

Many of our fondest memories of childhood consist of 'special days out' as a family 'treat' where everybody was taken to on a family outing to a new and exciting place. Again, it doesn't really matter what it is, or even if it is only a picnic in the country and you just played French Cricket or Frisbee afterwards, it's the sense of occasion that matters and that everybody is involved in the preparation, participation and packing up afterwards. Organising such trips makes sure that at least some weekends and bank holidays are remembered as significant events rather than a blur of 'Slobsessions' spent crashed in SKY-pilot mode interspersed by occasional forays to **Macyuckville**.

Exercise 7

Are we there yet?

1. In the table below, tick off the venues that you have visited as a family.
2. Ask your wife/partner which of the unticked venues SHE would like to visit next.
3. Agree a date in the family diary to have a family 'Treat' and then actually do it.
4. Deduct a Mark if you had a major family row.
5. Earn a bonus mark if you return with all the children and pets you set out with.

Venue	Local	National	International
Arranged Game (eg Bowling)			
Castle or Stately Home			
Cinema			
Circus			
Concert			
Fairground or Carnival			
Farm			
Lake or River			
Moorland or mountain			
Museum			
Park			
Picnic			
Spectator Sport (eg Football)			
Theatre or Pantomime			
Theme Park			
Zoo			

We're all going on a Summer Holiday

Summer holidays form an integral part of the memory-bank of childhood and are times of the year when your children should be able to count on a block booking for some undiluted attention from Mum and Dad. You probably have your own memories of squatting on a windswept, barely sunny beach at Bognor/Harlech/Scarborough/Blackpool where, with bucket and spade you built a castle with your own Dad. If you relate this to your wife, SHE will smile gently and respond with "Oh yes, we always used to go to….."

It is now your turn to create similar memories for your own offspring. Your range of holidays will probably be determined by your own interests, your available finances and the current capabilities of the rest of the family. You will never take the hassle out of going on holiday as a family, but you can reduce it to manageable proportions by applying some simple principles:

1) Plan early. Make sure that the hotel/apartment/villa has facilities suitable for a family with children in your age range – how many steps up to the door? Is a cot provided? Do they have a crèche, games room and a specific children's swimming pool. When did you last check the passports – have the children got passports? What about medical insurance or an E111 form if you are going abroad ?

2) Book a child–friendly holiday appropriate to your children's age. If they are Leg Limpets, then postpone the skiing holiday and hit the beach; if they are 'tweenies, find a 'family resort' that offers a wide range of activities and venues nearby and, if they are teenage Gangly Lions, then reconsider the whole enterprise altogether or make it an Action Holiday that is going to knacker them physically, widen their horizons and challenge their perceptions of you and the world.

3) Can you go with others? Scan your address book to see if there is another family with whom you get on well who have children of the same age who might be interested in sharing the childcare.

4) Essentials. Take gallons of Factor 60 suntan lotion and make sure that each child has taken at least one travel game and a couple of books, check the Family Travel Insurance for paediatric cover and make sure that EVERYBODY knows that at least one hour a day is designated as "Daddy's Quiet Time" when he is NOT to be disturbed.

5) Leave your mobile/Blackberry/laptop at home. You really don't need to check that everything's OK in the office – that's what delegation and empowerment are about. Be confident enough to let it all go for a little while and really recharge your batteries. Besides if it all does go to pot while you're away, they'll appreciate you more when you get back and it'll be a good chance to talk about that pay-rise you think you deserve.

6) Homeward bound. Whatever you do and wherever you go, make certain that 'Blankie'/'Teddy'/'Mr Wiggles' is in the car/suitcase/rucksack before you set off homewards. It will be YOUR fault, come what may, if that favourite 'person' is left behind . SHE will have no mercy!

'Precious Time'

"The most important thing you can give your children is your time."

When you do manage to find time to learn how to play again, you will find that you will have an escalating number of claims on your time from the junior members of the family, as well as a never-ending list from Mum. You MUST ensure that you share out your time and energy to ensure that everybody gets a bit. It is important that each Little Person gets their own share of you, because they will notice and they will demand their due allotment. It is too easy to spend your time following a favourite sport/team with a child who displays an allied interest or in supporting one who shows early potential as a future David Beckham, Johnny Wilkinson or Sharon Davies. However, you have a duty as a Dad to find some common ground with every child, or to learn about their favourite hobby/sport in order to give them their fair share of your time and energy. This under-fulfilment is most probably going to occur with your daughter(s), so learn the rules and tactics of Netball, Hockey or Lacrosse as early as possible and urge her to join a Beach Volleyball Club with the possibility of a scholarship in Santa Barbara, California or Bondi Beach, Sydney when she is in her early twenties so that you get some positive payback in the future.

"Well he was so good that we decided to send him back as the manager of the Santa Barbara ladies beach volleyball team."

Good Reasons for Not Doing Things.

There are times however, when a good excuse can come in handy for NOT doing things, for instance, when England are poised to kick off in the Grand Slam final match of the Six Nations against France. Little People and their Mums have a curious knack of wanting things JUST when you want to be totally left alone. In the absence of Vaseline to grease the playroom door or a handful of green Smarties to throw onto the garden lawn, try some of this repertoire of excuses:

I've got a bone in my leg.
I have to go back to the Gooseberry Bush where we found you and make sure that there's no-one else waiting to be picked up.

My skin's too thin and my blood will spill out onto the carpet if I move too far this afternoon.

My ears are flapping and I haven't stuck them back properly.

I'm just checking the insides of my eyelids for cracks.

The eyes in the back of my head are tired and need a rest.

The Rugby/Football is on and though I don't want to, I've promised Grandpa that I would watch it and tell him how they got on.

There's a duck over there trying to show me how well he can swim.

My legs are worn out and I'm waiting for the Postman to bring me some new ones.

The birds in the garden have asked me to a meeting to discuss their wages

I am doing something, XXXX (insert name of Leglimpet/Tweenie) and

Mummy and I are just snuggling up together here for a few minutes 'Precious Time'.

And finally…

Because I'm the Daddy and I say so (and Mummy agrees).

Homework:

During the next week:

1. Spend at least One Hour playing with each of your children.
2. Take out a Board Game and play it with all of your children. (Separate task to above). Make sure that there are no pieces that are likely to be eaten or chewed by very Little People or else choose a different game.
3. Allocate a specific period of time to each child to follow one of their activities (Football, Model-making, Basketball, Ballet/ Dancing)
4. Sit down and have 'Tea' with the Little People
5. Have Sunday Lunch as a 'real' meal (with proper manners and NO TV)
6. Sit with a Little Person and draw moustaches, beards and spectacles on everybody in the newspaper. You'll know you're having fun when they start drawing nits into the politician's hair. Spend the next hour, checking their hair for nits.
7. Find Out where the Local Library is located and get them registered for a Library Card. (Bonus mark if you get a Library Card for yourself as well).

Educating Daddy

Part Two - The Middle Ages

A guide to 'tweenies

Educating Daddy

The Middle Ages
'tweenies

These intermediate chapters are for those of you who have experienced the delight of being a Daddy of Leg Limpets but who have not yet endured the frustration of being a father of teenagers. You have progressed to the Middle Ages, where your Little People are 'inbetweenies', or 'tweenies for short. They have moved up from babyhood but are definitely nowhere near adulthood. It is a time of great imagination and exploration, and the person they most want to lead them is YOU. You are at the zenith of your position as my Dad, THE Dad, even THE BEST DAD IN THE WORLD. Never again will you be held in such esteem by anybody else – so enjoy it, because it only lasts for about five to seven years. There's a lot of fun to be had doing all the things that you always wanted to do, but that your own Mum never let you.

During this period there is a danger that you will just unconsciously accept their presence and get on with your family life, incorporating them only where and when it is most convenient. After all, they are now fully mobile, semi-literate, capable of fending for themselves amongst their peers and reasonably good at scavenging if you are not there to drag a mammoth back to the cave. However, if you miss this opportunity, then you will miss out on one of the great joys of being a Dad, that of teaching and socialising your children. When you look back through the mental photo album of your children, you'll wonder why all the pictures of them from about seven to 12 years old are blurred and why you have no clear memory of what they did. This is when they learn all about the world that surrounds them. They need you now more than ever on moral, mental and physical levels.

At the same time, you have to set the foundations for their development as adults. If they are left to roam the streets unrestrained, abusing people or property then they will turn into problem teenagers. So save yourself and society the hassle in the next few years and put in the investment in time and effort now. It will be worth it...

Educating Daddy

6
Planting and Pruning the Money Tree

Considering your investment

"Your children are your most precious possession. So treasure them."

You cannot afford to have children. Nobody can. However, since they have now entered your life forever, you will have to find a way to pay for them. No matter how hard you work, you will find that your available money seems to disappear in a never-ending round of 'must haves' like food, housing, clothes, books, shoes, and toys. If there is anything left, then the cost of the family holiday will wipe the slate totally clean even before you leave the rain-swept shores of the British Isles.

"The pace at which you buy toys increases in direct proportion to however much you seem to earn."

The bankruptcy rollercoaster begins with the 'start-up costs' of cot, baby clothes, pram/stroller, bottles/feed steriliser, changing mat, car seat and the multitude of adorable, but utterly useless, stuffed animals and cartoon characters that you will be trying to get rid of for the next 20 years. The next biggest input cost in the 21st Century is disposable nappies, which could seemingly provide the basis for another continent bridging the gap between Europe/Africa and the Americas (the Incontinent, perhaps?).

You should cheer loudly on the day that your child becomes 'dry through the night' because the savings will be enough to fund its university education if you switch the equivalent cost into a building society account from that day forward. The spending spree continues mercilessly as your children insist on growing, despite all your best efforts to shoehorn them into the same set of clothes for yet another season.

Growing bills

The pace at which you buy clothes, books, toys and (in this modern age) software seems to increase in direct proportion to however much you seem to earn. The surge of delight when your children first speak is rapidly diminished when you realise they are merely trying to ask you for more money and their cuddles are covert pat-you-downs in search of your wallet or pocket-change. The bigger they get, the more expensive their tastes; fashions have to be followed and peer groups encourage them to pressurise parents into further expenditure. The toys get bigger, as do the prices and the repair bills and we haven't even begun to talk about the costs of computers and internet access or telephone and/or mobile phone bills.

In the 21st Century world, they are constantly receiving targeted messages that tell them that they are not 'cool' or 'with it' unless they wear, eat, see, speak, drive and holiday in a certain manner. How they respond to this barrage of advertisement, much of it unconsciously absorbed through product placement or 'timely' advertising, is down to you and your partner. It is up to you to manage their expectations and not allow the television/internet/media and the ad agencies to do it for you. But you will have to be firm, consistent and very resilient to manage them effectively.

Child cost benefit analysis

Let us do a rough cost benefit analysis of the amount of money you could reasonably expect to spend per child. The exact amount that you spend on your children will, of course, ultimately depend upon your overall income. Estimates vary, but even the most conservative guesses place the cost of raising a child at £140,398[3] (between birth and 18 years of age) and that's without adding on anything for a University education or help with the first car. When you are considering the conception of your next child, just note that the cost of an average house in the UK in 2004 is £137,800[4] and ask your present child "Would you want a brother or sister or a house?"

Many young people cannot get onto the first rung of the property ladder now that first-time buyers need about £20,000 as an initial deposit, and consequently end up living at home for much longer, thus the true cost of raising children over the next 20 years is likely to be much larger. At the risk of scare-mongering, your major problem in years to come is not going to be in providing for them in the intervening years, but in working out how to get rid of them once they have grown up.

They do come cheaper by the dozen of course, because you can recycle clothes, toys and bathwater, but the incremental saving per child is only about £30,000 and, if you have three or more, you get a Summer Sales Saving of about £55,000 per child. This horrific realisation can seem manageable if you view it as an item of annual expenditure of about £7,800, or £150 per week or £21.50 per day, but even so you're going to have to plan how you're going to pay for them all. Just to put things into their proper perspective, just imagine yourself as Chairman Mao Tse Tung doing the same equation – no wonder he had bags under his eyes.

Exercise 8:

£21.50's worth of money well spent?

Look lovingly at your little ones and work out whether you had your £21.50's worth of value out of each of them today. Imagine what else you could have done with £150 per week (post tax), or £147 and 'a packet of three'.

"Hugs and cuddles cost nothing, so give them freely."

"One lady owner, low mileage, a few light bumps and scratches but very economical. Who'll give me 20 denarii?"

The Money Pit

So where's all this money going? Years two to five cost the most. The most expensive years for raising a child in a typical two–parent household in the UK are between the ages of one to five.[5]

First year = £7,138
Years 2-5 = £39,557
Years 6-11 = £31,000
Years 12-18 = £33,747
Years 19-21 = £30,000

Planting and pruning the money tree

And the largest expenditure items over the different life-stages of a child are:

First year: nursery furniture & equipment and child care
Years 2-5: child care
Years 6-11: recreation and food
Years 12-18: food and clothes
Years 19-21: education

The overall essentials and incidentals needed include:

1) Housing: Your current house/apartment is too small or will become so very shortly. So, whether you are paying rent or paying off a mortgage, you are certainly going to find the cost of it rising soon, unless you can downsize by moving from a small flat in Knightsbridge to a bigger place in rural Northamptonshire.

2) Fixtures and Fittings: Having acquired your extra living space you are now going to fork out a fortune to clutter it up with lots of new fixtures and fittings: a changing table, a high chair, extra shelves, a toy box, more beds/bunks/a cot etc etc. Offset this against the savings in beer money/romantic meals out if it makes you feel any better. It won't. If you have any money left, consider investing in shares in Fisher-Price or the Early Learning Centre since you will be contributing much towards their profit margins over the next few years.

3) Food: One can eat as cheaply as two, but three or more can't, especially when one of you needs special milk formula or baby food. As they become older, weekly supermarket trips have to be supplemented by additional raids on the local shop for MORE bread, milk, cereals, Cheesestrings....until they become teenagers, when they orbit round the house stopping off to suck up the entire contents of the refrigerator in an afternoon and the household food bill becomes astronomic as a consequence.

4) Hardware and Software: You will need more of everything: washing
powder, soap, shampoo, toothpaste, loo rolls, nappies, and batteries for a
whole host of things that you never even suspected you needed before you
had children.

5) Clothes: Grab your address book and work out the children's ages of all of
your family and friends. You now need to set up your own children's clothes
exchange to offset the volume of apparel that you are going to need. Once
they become fashion-conscious you can forget it, since everything will have to
be new and up to speed – unless of course you still have access to your artistic
mother-in law's 1960's wardrobe. This will never go out of fashion because it
was 'so individual' anyway.

6) Day care/Babysitters: Day care is only viable for dual income parents if
you have less than two children – unless of course you are running the Day
Care centre in which case the opposite is true. Good babysitters are to be treasured - but not too closely during the lift home.

7) Education: If you opt for private education you can expect to pay about
£8,000 per year for Prep School and up to about £20,000 per year for a full
boarding public school. If you can find a decent State run school, then you will
most probably be supplementing it with additional activity classes: tennis,
music, swimming lessons as well as football/rugby/judo or other sports clubs
all of which will need specialist equipment, a personal taxi service and lots of
your time.

8) Entertainment: Outside school and sleep, you will also need to keep your
child occupied with some form of constructive, and hopefully educational or
beneficial, activity – otherwise they will drive you bonkers with an incessant
whine of "I'm bored, what can I do now?" This wail will emanate from them at
least three times a day during school holidays, no matter what you do. You will
therefore need toys, books, videos, computer games, drawing materials
(unless you have a passion for regular interior decorating) and a healthy

savings account to fund it. Then, you will also have the external entertainment to account for: cinemas, football matches, museums, theme parks, and zoos, - all with the hidden cost bombshell of fizzy drinks, burgers/pizzas, sweets and a plethora of carbohydrate contributors to the obesity that plagues Generation XL.

9) Travel and Holidays: If you thought the house was too small, just wait until you look at the car again. It is constantly amazing how, as a bachelor, you could get an week's worth of luggage onto the parcel shelf in your open-topped sports car; you twitched when your partner showed you her baggage train and you will positively die when you see the paraphernalia needed for your latest family addition. Add to that the need for an additional seat on every aeroplane, train or boat that you travel on in future, with its consequent full-fare ticket and another room per pair of children, and the costs of a family holiday become seriously demoralising each time you venture over your own threshold.

10) Life Insurance: Make absolutely sure that you have some. All banks, building societies or mortgage companies will insist that any loans they make to you are covered by life insurance policies that will cover the cost of their outlay if you die. You could take the view, therefore, that at least your wife and children will have the house and/or car if you should inadvertently pop your clogs too early. However, you still need to ensure that they are going to be looked after until they can either find some sort of regular income for themselves or convert your collective assets to do so. We advise that you consult a properly registered Financial Services Advisor to tell you which products offer you what returns and cover – and remember that all of them are there to sell you something, nobody works for free and the final choice is yours. But, the responsibility for provision for your dependents is also yours. It would be much better to look down from your cloud content that your loved ones were well provided for, than to have them wishing you a warmer reception because you left them to live their own daily Hell. (And no, we were NOT insurance salesmen in our former lives)

*"...and to my sons, I leave my collector's set of 'Debbie Does Dallas'
and my annual subscription to 'Fetish Weekly'. May they enjoy..."*

Making a Will

If you haven't already made a will, then you should certainly think about it
now. You might have thought about doing so when you set up house with your
current wife or partner and, if so, then well done. BUT did you
actually get round to doing it? Part of your responsibility for your Little People is
to ensure that they will be looked after when you die.

You're probably saying 'Why bother? If I die, then my wife/partner will
inherit everything anyway!' Which is true, but what if you and your partner die
at the same time? Who is then going to inherit all of your estate and, more
importantly, who is going to look after your children, cats/dogs, and goldfish?

If you die without making a will, then you die 'intestate', which means that
your estate goes into a state of Limbo until the Courts decide who should
rightfully inherit it. The inherent consequences of this are that your estate cannot be touched to support your offspring until it is released by the Courts, your
heirs might not be who you would want them to be, and a reasonable

percentage of whatever you do leave will get eaten up in Court charges and lawyers' fees. If you own your own house and it has a total value, along with the rest of your property, of greater than £265,000 then your heirs will probably also be liable to Inheritance Tax, so you would do as well to also consult a financial tax planner or else you will be leaving 60% of your goods to your heirs and 40% to the Chancellor.

You can make your own will, even if you have to carve it into the dashboard of the car with your keys as the canal waters rise inexorably towards the roof of the vehicle and the seatbelt continues to be stubborn in releasing. Or, you can ask a lawyer to simply draft one for you. Just make sure that you include and/or consider the following items:

1) **A named executor** who will have the responsibility for making sure that your will is carried out properly. You can name your wife or partner to be your executor, but it is best to make sure that there is someone else nominated as well, just in case your wife/partner dies before or with you.

2) **Nominate a Guardian** for your children so that you can rest easy that someone who loves and cares for them will take over where you inadvertently left off until they become adults. Make sure that you ask whoever you are nominating first, so that it doesn't come as too much of a shock along with the news of your untimely demise.

3) **A clear statement of who should inherit what.** If you want to leave specific items or gifts to special people, or even Battersea Dogs' Home, then you will need to make special mention of them in the will.

4) **Make sure that you get it witnessed.** You should get at least two copies and at least two or three independent witnesses, who should NOT be mentioned in the will. Make sure that you send a copy to each of your executors and possibly leave one with your lawyer if you have used one. Make sure you keep a copy for yourselves and store it safely away where it cannot get lost/stolen or even burned accidentally.

5) **Think about updating it** when you have more children OR if you get divorced OR if you win the Lottery. Remember to collect in the copies of any old wills you have stored or distributed – or else the lawyers will have another heyday in sorting out which will is valid.

"If you don't sort out your Will, then a Lawyer Will."

How Money Works

An important part of the life cycle of any tree is to ensure the continuity of its genus. The Money Tree is no exception and an essential part of your job is to ensure that your children learn early on about the value of things and where they come from – especially if you don't want your Little People to be still living off you when they're Big People. Little People value things more when they've

How money really works

earned them and treasure their possessions more when they've had to pay for them or contribute towards them. The easiest way to introduce the basic concepts of economics is to let them earn an allowance through helping round the house and garden. You'll pay for their sweets, cinema tickets and clothes anyway – so make a bonus out of teaching them the value of money at the same time. Opening a building society account for them and making a fuss about 'going to make a deposit in their bank' is also an excellent method of showing them how to invest and where money comes from if they want to buy things for themselves. If you're lucky, by the time they become Gangly Lions they will have stashed enough to pay for all the 'cool' kit they're going to want – or enough to offset the cost of the university anyway.

Daddy's Tax

At the earliest stages, you should also introduce them to the concept of 'Daddy's Tax', which is an automatic levy where you get back a small bit of whatever they have managed to persuade you to buy them. This is a good introduction to the principle of taxation that they are going to experience for the rest of their lives anyway. It's also a useful way for you to get back at least one block of chocolate off the end of the bar. Like the real Inland Revenue, never allow them to default and pursue them for payment with a vicious ruthlessness that would impress Genghis Khan - you are, after all, only imitating real life and preparing them for it. With time you can refine the art by adding in stealth taxes on everything they do, but you might think about drawing a line when they get their first girlfriend or boyfriend.

"Your children will never learn about charity if they never see you practising it."

Charity

Whilst we are discussing the passage of money, it is worthwhile making sure that your Little People recognize how lucky they are in comparison to others. If you are reading this in the relatively peaceful comfort of a western democratic suburb with a manageable mortgage, connected utilities, central heating and a fridge full of food, then thank God for your luck and your ancestors for their blood, sweat and tears. Cast a thought for those less well off than you and donate your time, skills, effort and/or money in improving their lot by just a teensiest bit this year. Even better, make sure that you incorporate charity into your Dadhood by doing something that all of the family can be involved in —even if it is just cheering you across the finish line and covering you with a foil blanket as you're loaded into the ambulance. The ancient proverb states that "charity begins at home" because that is where you learn it best and where you are shown how to export it into your dealings in the wider world. Charity is habit-forming and doing something for others is a habit best learned from Mums and Dads who practise it naturally and regularly. You might think about choosing a family charity focus for the year and varying it annually, so that you widen your Little People's view of all the different deserving causes that there are in the charity marketplace.

Homework

Charity begins at home

1. Check that you and your wife/partner have made legal wills. If you have already made a will check that it properly reflects your current marital status, provision for children (and step-children), and has specified guardians should anything happen to you and your wife/partner.

2. Introduce your children to the concept of Daddy's Tax. Ensure that you practise it regularly.

3. Choose a charity for the year that you wish to do something for, or ask your children what they would choose as a family charity for the year. Organise an event to raise some sponsorship money for your charity and make sure that each child participates or has a specific role to play in the event.

7
The Walking Encyclopaedia

Tall Tales for Little People

Despite your Mother-in-Law's firmly held belief that you know nothing of any worth, to a Little Person you are a walking encyclopaedia. As the Dad, you will be expected to know all the answers to all of their questions. As if that were not enough, you will also be expected to be able to tell them how you know all the answers. Attendance at Daddy's College and demonstration of your Graduation Certificate is generally accepted by Little People as clear proof of both source and breadth of knowledge. Use this response often and with great authority and it can be extended well into the early twenties or thirties when they should apply for attendance themselves.

"Little People love to know how things work."

The normal questions that get asked first are those that are the most apparent and wonderful to the junior mind: "Why is the sky blue?" "Why is the sea blue?" And "Where does God live?" For those of you who have never yet found a satisfactory solution to these conundrums, the answers are (1) Because the painters go out early in the morning and paint it blue (clouds are the bits they missed) (2) Because the blue paint drips down from the sky when it rains and (3) at Number 42, Arcadia Gardens, Edendale, North Yorkshire.

Tall tales for Little Folk are great fun for both of you but they do rely upon Dads having both a ready wit, a wild imagination and the gall to propose mad solutions with a straight face to innocent minds. If they ask you where you got all this knowledge from tell them that at Daddy's College you were taught to use your three I's: **Imagination**, **Invention** and the **Internet**.

However, we do suggest that you have a back-up plan of using the truth in case you have actually spawned a micro-Einstein and wish to retain some form of paternal credibility. For the neuro-surgeons amongst you, the real answers are of course: (1) Refraction (2) Reflection and (3) Number 42A, Arcadia Gardens, Edendale, North Yorkshire.

Educating Daddy

Exercise 9

Reference Library

(1) You have two minutes to collect a dictionary, an encyclopaedia and an atlas from anywhere within your house. Internet access to them does NOT count and a point should be deducted for even thinking that they might be replaced by an online version. If you don't have these three essential items already, then let Father Christmas know.

(2) Excepting Antarctica, name three countries from each continent along with their capital cities and a famous product or person for each country. Score a bonus mark for each member of the family who can complete the exercise without using any of the essential reference books you have collected.

(3) Hints for Dads are included (although they may not all be 'helpful'), but you don't want to lose face when your 'tweenie completes the table in under two minutes whilst you and the Gangly Lions are still wondering whether Burkina Faso is a person or place or new alcopop.

Continent	Country	Capital	Famous For?
Africa	Ethiopia	Addis Ababa	SHE who must be obeyed/Black Hawk Down
	Mali	Timbuktu	The place to go in Deepest Africa (if you are 6)
	Upper Bongoland	Tarzania	Coconuts and Coups don't count. Try Oil
North America	USA	Hollywood	Land of the Free and Obese
	Canada	Quebec	Mounties and Shania Twain
	Texas	Houston	Big steaks and big heads
South America	Mexico	Mexico City	Cheap Labour and Tequila
	Brazil	Brasilia	Football and Nuts
	Chile	Santiago	Tasty mince and beans
Asia	India	Delhi	Taj Mahal and Gastroenteritis
	China	Beijing	Great Wall – no ceiling
	Japan	Tokyo	A G8 nation that still makes things.
Australasia	Australia	Canberra	Sheep, Surf and Sheilas
	New Zealand	Aukland	Land of the Rings
	Papua New Ginea	Port Moresby	Headhunters
Europe	England	London	Land of the Freebie
	Germany	Berlin	Beer, sausages, expensive cars
	France	Paris	Kiss, head and hairy armpit

It all depends on your point of view.

*"Education can never be taken from you
and you should never give it up."*

Schools and Schoolwork

Of course, real education is a thing that Mum will never leave to chance. She will take a close interest in it, knowing that if it was left up to Dad then Mankind would soon revert to searching for Witchety grubs (the larva of Xyleutes Leuchmochla Turn) and new ways to draw naked women on the walls of the cave. Lots of real education can be done around the house and garden and in daily routine, which is how most Mums start the process anyway. However, you can, and should, do your bit to ensure that the Little People are capable of reading you the newspaper when your eyesight fails and can count out your allowance once the pension runs out. So, make sure that you take your share of

A bedtime story will normally put them to sleep....

the bedtime reading, and try NOT to fall asleep on their bed whilst you do so - hands up all Dads who have done that already?

Your role in your children's education should reflect your roles as a Dad (Protector, Provider, Lawmaker, Teacher). You can help prepare them to go to school by soothing their worries and holding their hand during the first few, awesome, days. You should help pick the right school for them and support them while they are there. Be there for sports matches and school plays, attend parent/teacher meetings and prove that although "My Dad's bigger than Your Dad ", you don't need to settle it with fisticuffs. You need to take time out to meet their teachers and complement their curriculum, whilst noting how much of it has changed since you were at school. You will have to be adept at spotting when they have a problem, which could be social, political, technical or even financial, and be able to help them to work out a solution. Your greatest contribution is probably going to be in making sure they do their bit when they are at school and that they do their homework when they're not. Homework will be a thorny issue that slowly escalates as the burden gets greater through their school years. Try to get them into the habit of doing homework at a regular time, in a quiet place and with your help if needed. You'll be amazed by how much you can remember and horrified by how much you have forgotten. They will be amazed by how much you know and horrified that you haven't forgotten that they had homework to do in the first place.

Reading the school report

Once a Term they will come home with a School Report or Progress Report. Make it a formal occasion, without quite elevating to that of 'the Final Judgement', where you as The Dad sit down with them in a quiet corner and read it through with them. Not only does it tell you how they are doing, but it should also prompt you to ask yourself what else you can do to help in areas where they are finding difficulty in understanding or keeping up. The most important thing is that they will recognize that you care how well they are doing at school and that you take an active interest in their work. They already know that Mum cares about what they do at school, because she's the one who normally takes them and picks them up again or goes in at parents' evenings or if/when they get into trouble. But they need to know that you care as well, and that you are willing to take steps to ensure that they do as well as they can with

their natural abilities. Wouldn't it be great if your boss did the same to you?

Get them to practise their mental maths whilst you are doing the shopping in the supermarket. Put a map of the world on the wall and plot where you/SHE and they have been and where you might go one day and involve new countries into your games. Do a jigsaw together or build a spaceship in the garage and take a quick orbit to point out the continents and be back in time for tea. Alternatively, just spend the day out at the National Gallery, Natural Science Museum or the Smithsonian. You'll soon find that one question will prompt another and exploring books for the answers can be both good fun and a great way to get to know your children better. Oh, and by the way, Who does fire shooting stars? Why do angels have wings? And, do lawyers really have no Dads?

Lessons in Safety

The other major element of 'How things Work' is a safety brief for your Little People. Of course this has to be a gradual process to explain things as they encounter them, but you will be horrified by how many ways there are around your house and garden to kill, maim or seriously hurt your children - if you stop to think about it. Child-proofing your home is really quite easy, though it takes a little thought and time, and requires the occasional use of your DIY toolkit.

Your child is pre-programmed from birth to explore and try everything remotely interesting around him/her. This normally consists of putting anything that can be picked up into their mouths and thus you must be on guard for dog bowls, cat litters, dropped screws/washers/nuts and anything else that YOU might take for granted, but is novel, fascinating and potentially nutritious to a Leg Limpet. They do learn quickly, helped by trial and error, but you will need to be watchful once they start to get mobile around the six month mark. Thereafter, you will have to 'raise the bar' as your toddler grows in stature and reach and as he/she learns new skills like climbing or running. Fires and radiators can easily be seen and felt as a source of danger and hurt, but electricity is a more difficult danger to point out and for the child to understand. Ideally, make sure that your house is fitted with a circuit-breaker that will not allow for full human connection to the mains and you should make a special effort to make sure that all reachable sockets either have a pin-cover or a plug inserted into them. Where possible try to position furniture or covers in front of sockets so that they don't become an attraction to a young inquisitive mind and fingers. You should also make sure that the connecting cables are tucked away out of sight because babies like puppies, are not too particular about what they are chewing on when they are teething.

The main hazards (Thingies) to be aware of are:

- Toxic substances – remembering that most Little People cannot read labels.
- Hot and Heavy objects – especially if pulled off shelves or worktops.
- Ingested items that can be put in the mouth but which can choke.
- Notable/knot-able cords that just hang about the place.
- Glass or other breakables that produce splinters or shards.
- Incendiaries and other things that burn.
- Electricity, batteries and anything connected to the mains.
- Sharp objects like knives, screwdrivers or scissors.

Exercise 10

SAFETY PIN

Get on your hands and knees and crawl round the house from room to room looking at the house from a child's point of view. Look for thingies, reach for thingies, touch thingies, pull thingies and child-proof as you go. It will astonish you to find out how many dangerous thingies you have lying around the house.

A word of warning though: ensure that the neighbours and the postman do not see you completing this exercise or else you will find yourself the butt of all good humour for the next decade. Alternatively, sell tickets and donate the proceeds to a good children's charity. (A bonus mark if you can persuade your wife/partner to take part in this exercise as well).

"NO" means "NO"

Of course domestic life has to keep going on a daily basis and you cannot stop just because you now have a toddler around, but you will have to start by putting everything firmly away, out of reach of little fingers, once it has been used. Child safety locks are a great modern idea and are very useful for about the first three to four years on fridges and any drawers that are at an 'interesting' height. However, the best child-safety lock is inserted mentally by you and Mum into the brain of your Little People from as early an age as possible: - "NO means NO". Even babies will learn very early on from the volume and tone of your voice that a sharp "NO!" is a warning of danger. This can be expanded upon later by words such as "Sharp", "Hot" or "Ouch" or "Bleaucch!" and a grimace to reinforce the message that they are likely to come to harm if they continue with that course of action. Most Little People will understand and obey quite quickly and, if you naturally continue the process as they grow, they'll not only absorb the basic rules but begin to apply them to new experiences as they get older. For instance, how many of us remember the fight for Human Rights when the wearing of seat belts became legally enforceable but now delight when we see our own children automatically and naturally click themselves in when they get in the car?

No Go Areas and May Go Areas

Whilst we are discussing cars, some items are too dangerous to be left out, so lock them away. Items such as cleaning products, bleaches, electrical drills and saws, fertilizers and pesticides, paint and paint strippers and, especially, guns and ammunition. However, if you have power tools on a workbench or just at hand when you are doing some DIY or repairs, little fingers will inevitably find them in that one moment when you are not looking so you might find it necessary to have a 'No Go Area' such as Dad 's workshop or shed which is padlocked and/or only entered in the company of an adult and never when the power's on.

The other possible MAY GO AREA is the 'beyond the front gate', and a rule of "if you go beyond it I want to know first" is always a useful one to implement as early as possible. Until then you should fit a solid, child-proof catch so that you precious Little People don't wander off without you knowing about it. When they get to be about 18, show them how to open it for themselves and venture out without asking your permission any longer.

Having frightened you Dads near to death by this catalogue of potential disaster, there remains only one more piece of advice on this topic: make sure that your home has a well stocked First Aid Kit that is kept in an obvious and easily reached (by an adult) location. When you need it, you won't want to have to search for it.

Work

"To you, work is a necessity. To them, it is a distraction."

No chapter on 'How Things Work' would be complete without a few words about work itself. After all, your Little People need to have some story to explain why you disappear every day and re-appear hours later totally knackered and in need of a serious drink before you play with them. You will have to explain what you do at work, where you do it and, perhaps, why you do it. It will help you considerably if you have a 'Take your child to Work' day so that they can see most of these things for themselves and you'll find that their Mum will often not mind coming as well – if only to check out the girls in accounts and ensure that your admin assistant really is 50+ in both girth and age. How you describe your occupation will help shape their views on work and what it means to them. Hopefully, you find your work an outlet for your creativity rather than a source of drudgery, but whatever your regard for it, you can be sure that your wife and children will know – even if you haven't actually iterated your feelings about it. If you feel you are only a 'drudge' – get a life and a new job, or get a creative outlet to balance the drudgery so that life is much more amusing for those around you.

And a final word on work: if you are a respected person at your place of work, make it clear that you have family responsibilities and when you need to leave work to look after your children, say so, don't pretend otherwise. Others will accept and follow your leadership. If you are an employee, find out whether you can work in more flexible and family-friendly ways - you may be able to use flexi-time or work from home - the more in control you are of your time, the easier it is to balance work and family life. And, if you are an employer or senior manager, make life easier for other Dads.

Homework

During the next week:

1) Build something with your child. (Model car/aeroplane/boat or dolls' house)
2) Take your child to an activity museum or backpack your Leg Limpet to a farmyard. (Bonus mark if you make all the farmyard noises).
3) Invent another tall tale (Eg: Why do fairies always live at the bottom of the garden? Why not at the top or the sides?) that makes your Little Person laugh out loud. (Bonus mark if Mum believes it as well and laughs – but not at you).
5) Make sure that you have swept the house for toxic items and have a separate (lockable) store cupboard for them.
6) There are also a wealth of good home/child-orientated first aid books available, so go out and buy one, read up on the basics or give your local St John's Ambulance a call to attend a basic first aid course.
7) Take your child to work or organise a visit to your office/workplace if your company doesn't already have a family day. (Oil rig workers might want to try a trip to the petrol station instead).

8
Making friends with your little people

Keeping Calm

The first thing to remember about your children is that, given a normal upbringing, they will love you, they may like you and, every so often, they might say that they hate you. The art of great Daddyhood is to guarantee the love, maximise the opportunities for liking one another and try not worry too much when they stamp off venting satanic verses. As a Dad, you will expect your children to keep up the standards that you set and will be appalled when they don't. However, don't expect them to grow up too quickly, because they won't and you'll just end up very disappointed wondering why you married a woman with a defective criminal gene that she's just passed on to your children. Be especially careful with your first-born, they're paving a path for both of you and neither of you has full visibility of the road plan. Throughout this book, and especially during this Chapter, remember you are their parent first and foremost. You'll be around them longer, love them more and watch out for them come

Why Buddha really sought Peace and Enlightenment....

what may, so be friendly by all means, but don't try to be popular. Blood is a lot thicker than water and they are sure to have lots of friends as they grow up, but they will only one set of real parents and even though they may not always recognise it, they need you more.

"Your children are with you for life, you will never be rid of them."

So, if they are going to be around for a long time, you'd better get to know them properly. How well do you think you know your own children? Try the following exercise to see how much real attention you've paid to them since they've been cluttering up your house and your well-ordered lifestyle. An interesting twist here is to make (Hah!) Mum do the same exercise at the same time and compare the tables whilst the children supply the real answers. You will certainly find out very quickly how easy it is to just assume that you are taking an interest in them, without really paying attention to the detail in their lives.

At the leg limpet stage, it is really easy to make and stay friends with your Little People. All it needs is your input because theirs will happen regardless. At this stage, friendship will be born out of intimacy and your participation in those events which are the central and most personal issues in their lives: feeding, changing, bathing and cuddling. When the bottle feeding begins, take a hand in the feeding rituals and earn yourself some serious Brownie Points from Mum. Have a Dad/Baby cuddling time on a Saturday afternoon, just about kick-off time, particularly since you cannot move for an hour or so because the baby might wake up. Take a major role in nappy changing, especially when your Leg Limpet becomes a toddler and you have to use persuasion, patience and imaginative distractions to keep the little Herbert amused while you get on with the 'jobbie' in hand.

At the 'tweenies stage, your Little People will be relatively easy to make friends with - so long as you spend time with them. This is easy to say but difficult to do, especially if you already have another new baby or two to amuse you. Take an interest in the three Rs and help with the homework – they will be amazed at this age by how much you know, so will Mum. Find a common ground in sport, music or a hobby; your Little People won't know what is possible so you

Exercise 11

Who the Heck are You?

For each of your children, name the items listed below. Whilst you may not wish to desecrate your Student Handbook with your wax crayon, you will be appalled by how few of these boxes you can fill in. Alternatively, you might be a Yorkshire farmer and wonder what all the fuss is about anyway. Warning: do not be disheartened if you can only answer the first three, you are after all only a Dad. If you cannot even manage the first three, however, consult your local Crime Prevention Officer: have you not wondered who all those short people tramping through in your house are?

ITEM	CHILD 1	CHILD 2	CHILD 3
Name			
Sex			
Birthday			
Favourite Toy (incl name)			
Favourite Book/Story			
Favourite Clothes			
Best Friend			
Favourite Colour			
Favourite Food			
Food they most dislike			
Favourite Game			
Favourite TV Programme			

Also answer the following questions about each child:
When was the last time you talked to them (and for how long)?
When was the last time you took them out (and where)?
When was the last time you watched them play in a match?
When was the last time you taught them something (and what was it)?
When was the last School Play they were in (+ Bonus if you were actually there)?

have to find it based on your perceptions of what they are like as children and what they are likely to be like as Big People. But tailor it to them not to you - after all, you don't want them to make the mistakes you made do you?

Educating Daddy

"Little People get VERY tired between 4 and 6 o' clock in the evening."

"So what?" you say. This is known as the 'Witching Hour' amongst the Mum-People, when the most important things in the universe are tea, bath and bed. Do not tamper with the workings of the domestic routine. It is a tank that rumbles irresistibly onwards, so do not stand in its way, and not try to alter its course, or you will get crushed! Learn to oil the works rather than throw a spanner in them. If you are at home at this time of night, there are some very simple rules: Little People are tired, have low sugar levels and need food, patience and distraction NOT rules, Daddy-Monsters and winding up. You are the novelty at this time of night, so learn how to cope with the barrage of immediate demands for your time and attention and, whatever you do, don't get cross.

"You are the Head of the House, but you don't have to prove it as soon as you come home from work."

When you come home, take the pressure off – don't add to it. Your contribution as a Dad is to deal with them with the patience that SHE has lost over the past few hours. Don't wind them up, help to wind them down instead. The older they get the more they need your influence and the more they will seek it, so be careful not to turn them away through not recognizing what they are really asking for – your time, your attention and your approval and love. Feel great about it – when the rest of the world hates you, your Little People will love you – but then, simple minds are very easily pleased and your nearest rival is a very tattered Blankie or 'First Bear'.

He or SHE who must be Obeyed?

There was a day when the ultimate threat was "Just wait until Dad gets home." More fathers these days are either working from home, or are using flexi-time to spend more of the day at home when the family are around. Times have changed but you will still find that in the majority of cases that somebody has to assume the mantle of lawmaker and as 'the Dad' it will probably be you.

But the fact that you lay down the law, shouldn't get in the way of your being friends with them – the best of friends will tell them honestly when they are wrong, just as much as they will support them when they are right. Leg limpets are too young to rationalise 'rules' and so a firm, and oft repeated, 'No' with a policy of redirection or distraction from the immediate danger will probably work best for the first few years. As your Little People grow into 'tweenies, you will have to start developing a clear basis for the behavioural rules that they will take with them through life.

Three Principles of Paternal Protection:

1) **Protect Your Children from themselves**, so that they don't lick a sharp knife, plug themselves into the mains, or walk under a bus.

2) **Protect Others from Your Child**, so that it doesn't become the 'demon child from hell' that nobody wants to let theirs play with.

3) **Protect Property**, so that they respect other people's things and know that you take a very firm line on vandalism or wanton destruction.

Homework:

During the next week:

1. Take the children to school and say hello to their class teacher. (Bonus mark if you ask how they are getting on in class.) Do not stop to chat her up! You will get spotted and you won't get any stars.
2. Watch them play in a match.
3. Read them their favourite book or listen to their favourite record.
4. Take them somewhere new that you haven't been to either.
5. Ask them to pick a letter of the alphabet and then teach them about something beginning with that letter. (A bonus mark if you can go through all 26 letters without losing their interest or having to resort to a reference book).

Educating Daddy

9

Work and Play for 'tweenies

Doing Your Fair Share – Parents NOT Slaves

If you have been following the advice given so far, you'll be used to the idea of children helping out with the chores and that your place in their life is not that of domestic slave. You won't be surprised that children will not naturally or voluntarily help around the house and will need to be trained before they do so willingly. As with the tasks you gave them when they were 'Leg Limpets' ensure that the jobs you give your 'tweenies are within their capability for their age.

For 'tweenies, enlarge the task so that they are doing more to keep their 'living space' tidy, and give them bigger jobs to do with you or Mummy: fold up the dry washing, help write out the shopping list, clear the table, put out the milk bottles, help wash the car, help weed the garden. You will find that you probably have to negotiate a remuneration scheme for 'extra' jobs, but treat it as another aspect of learning and growing – just don't let them bring in arbitrators or lawyers.

Games for 'tweenies - The Internet in a PC World

It is a tough job keeping up to date with the changes of the Interactive World these days. No sooner had you mastered your computer and accessed the Internet, but 'they' then invented Chat rooms, Instant Messaging and Texting. Just wait for Videostreaming. Computers and the Internet have opened up a whole new vista for your Little People. They can now travel further, hear, see and explore more places and things than was ever possible when you were their age. If they are not totally PC literate then they will be second class citizens in the world of tomorrow , which will be their world, and it is your responsibility to prepare them for it just as you would with Reading, 'Riting and 'Rithmatic. You can buy, or borrow from your local library, some truly great software that can help them with all stages of their education and complement their set curriculum whilst entertaining them as well. Note also though that there is a darker side to the educational interactive world where the less scrupulous offer pre-written dissertations or even exam-sitting prostitutes to lift the burden of learning from your darlings – at a price. Therefore, you and they need to be savvy as to what the Internet offers and what protection and advice your Little People need in using it. The internet is like bringing a city into your home: there are lots of exciting places to go and lots of things to do, but there are also lots of places that you wouldn't want them to go and some people you definitely don't want them to meet.

Internet dangers
The main dangers for children are:

1) Contact: Potentially from someone online who wishes them harm or who gains some form of gratuitous pleasure from your child. Children have to re-learn the Stranger = Danger maxim in a new context and NEVER give out their personal details or agree to meet alone with anyone they may have met on the Internet.

2) Content: Check out the sites they've visited and the material they have seen. Agree the ground rules about where they should go and how they should behave. Get them to apply their own inbuilt critic – but just as you'd watch them from afar across the park, check on them anyway through the Internet History button on the PC they use to access the Web.

3) Commercialism: There is some aggressive online marketing directed particularly at children which can invade a child's and your privacy. Discourage your children from filling in any forms which ask for personal details.

"You are the best filter for Internet access and content."

There are of course 'Filtering' programmes which can help to block a lot of inappropriate material and the best major Internet Service Providers (ISPs) will offer it as part of the access package for free. But they can never be 100%

effective, as the immoral and amoral will always be looking for ways round them, and they can never be a substitute for good parental supervision. Remember that your children have a number of other access points these days at school, at friends' homes, in the library, at youth clubs or just in high-street Internet Cafes so the best filter will be the inbuilt one that you attach to the best computer in the world - the permanently portable one between their ears. Take the time to find the best and most useful sites for them (eg www.bbc.co.uk for children's entertainment or educational back-up) and encourage them to stick to fun, positive sites that reinforce their interests or schoolwork. A SMART acronym for some useful internet safety rules is:

Safe: Be careful, don't give out your name, address, mobile phone number, school name or password to people you meet online.

Meeting: Anybody you have met in cyberspace can be dangerous. Only do so with parents' permission and then, only when they can be present.

Accept: Only accept e-mails or files which come from people you know well or trust. Otherwise they might contain viruses or nasty messages.

Remember: Always remember that anyone online might be lying about who they say they are and what they do. It is easy to log off or check out of a chat room.

Tell: Tell Mum or Dad if someone or something makes you feel uncomfortable.

The real victims of the Video Game

The next potential interactive horror comes in the form of the multiplicity of video games that are available for both Playstations, PCs and, soon, third generation mobile telephones. The software games industry protects itself by classifying them by content acceptability for escalating age groups but, in practice there is little, if any, real control over their sale or rental. You will be (or should be) utterly aghast one day when you accidentally pass your offspring and their friends sprawled in front of a screen laughing over some unfortunate that they have just pulled from his car, given a savage beating to prior to shooting him and then driven off at high speed ramming other pedestrians and vehicles during the getaway. Do not wonder where you went wrong in the intervening years when you are standing outside the Crown Court watching your pride and joy carted off to enjoy Her Majesty's Pleasure.

'Children do as Children see', and if they believe that it is acceptable to behave in such a way, and that you do NOT see it as wrong either, then they will be more inclined to try it out for real when they get into the big wide world outside. Moreover, when their popular models and current icons also reinforce the same virtual message through their public behaviour, and when we extol the virtues of games/behaviour on popular national youth oriented radio or television programmes, we give them a level of acceptability which is at odds with what we should want for our society of the future.

But if you have the absorbent mind of a child and you are barraged by such messages, reinforced by the apparent endorsement of your parents and guardians, what are you likely to believe and how are you likely to behave in the future? It's not a matter of parental intolerance or fuddy-duddy Colonel Blimpism, it's a matter of rationally matching current social education, even through virtual games, with our expectations for future social behaviour in real life. The new update for FIFA 2020 is likely to include optional extras for the striker (Feck'em) to shoot the ball under the crossbar, the defender (Feroneduz) to pass the drugs test and for the mid-fielders (Pokitt and Stuffah) not to join the traditional post-match spit roast with an under-aged, one-legged, Andalusian cheerleader.

Cards, games and books

Cards and board games will continue to be useful to 'tweenies, and everything we said about reading and leg limpets applies equally here. Especially for boys a male 'reading role model' may be a very useful way of encouraging the reading habit and of counter-acting the general trend of poorer literacy among boys than girls. If you have 'tweenies, then you will need to progress to books with chapters, fewer pictures and more words and, if you are really adventurous, get them to draw the pictures and then put a story together for them in a loose-leaved book that they can show their friends and relations.

Exercise 12

Playtime for Dads

Dads of Tweenies, need to go and build a 'den' with the help of children. It can be inside or outside, depending on the weather, country and traffic density of the Student Dad and his family, – just check it out with Mum regarding clothes and footwear beforehand. Added Bonus mark if the dog/cat/hamster is included and finds its way back to its bed without losing any limbs. Double Bonus marks if the same caveat can be applied to the children.

Exercise 13

Playtime in the School Holidays

You will have a fight at the beginning of every holiday period (No, that is NOT the exercise) when your children use the excuse of the holidays to initiate the Audiovisual Insatiability Motor. Negotiate, from a position of parental authority, that they spend at least 30 minutes doing some active pastime first. The preferred range and order of activities is to do:

Something Physical,
Something Musical,
Something Mental,
Something Creative,
And only then Something Electrical

Notes:

1. Snogging your girlfriend/boyfriend does NOT count as something physical or creative.
2. Listening to CDs does NOT count as something musical.
3. Reading a Book does count as something mental.
4. Something Electrical = TV, video, DVD, CD, PlayStation, Computer or Internet.
5. Non-compliance should be met by removal of privileges – or in extremis (temporary) removal of the offending electronic device.

Educating Daddy

Part Three - The Senior Terms

A guide to 'Gangly Lions'

The Senior Terms
'Gangly Lions'

These latter Chapters are akin to shining a torch up the Teenage Tunnel. They should show you the rough direction, outline the walls and can be used to illuminate specific issues, but you'll still need to be careful how you tread because some of the things you come across will leave a nasty smell and some of them could even mark you for life. Of all the zones of Dadhood, this is the most difficult - for you and for them.

All things in life are in balance. Where you have experienced the zenith as the Daddy Deity to Leg Limpets and 'tweenies, you will now experience the nadir as 'Perceived Paternal Plankton'. In the short duration of a 13th birthday party you and Mum will have become the most embarrassing people in the world. Your dress sense is pitiful, your music is lamentable, your style is medieval, you are a reactionary fascist and your rules are authoritarian.

The fact that you sleep with their mother is both personally offensive and absolutely disgusting. Any thought or mention of sex is utterly horrifying and you can clear a room of teenagers faster than a flatulent labrador by having a good snog with your wife/partner in front of them. If you want to really gross them out try saying: "Shall we use tongues as well darling?" It is amazing to them that geriatric euthanasia for the over 30 year olds wasn't put on the statute books in the mid-1960s and, if you try dancing or any form of PDA (public display of affection) then they will probably run a campaign to institute it forthwith.

In short, you know nothing and understand even less, which is mathematically impossible but entirely credible to the adolescent brain. You are acceptable only in your roles as sometime Computer technician, Taxi-driver or Paymaster General. Grit your teeth, if you have any left, and see a good dentist regularly because there will be much gnashing and wailing over the next few years.

Discipline or Domination?

It is no longer enough just to rely on your status as the Dad Person when they become Gangly Lions. After years of playing the Omniscient Benefactor of their Universe for about their first dozen years, their image of you begins to crumble as they begin to move (metaphorically) into the 'House' of their Mentor. At this stage they have observed you long enough to know that you are human and compare you not only with other examples around, but also with themselves. Your sons will begin to win the sprints, you begin to struggle to win the arm-wrestling and you have to resort to old Army tricks to control them in impromptu rough and tumble sessions.

Meanwhile, your daughters begin to develop long limbs, unnerving bumps in all the right places and 'friends' who are more interested taking your daughter to all the wrong places. No more are you the Daddy Deity of their earlier years, who was seldom questioned, (nearly) always obeyed and frequently hugged. It is time for you to develop your relationship into one that will, hopefully, last you a lifetime. You will need to earn their respect and friendship rather than relying on a simplistic filial relationship based on a shared genetic inheritance and two minutes of lust, slippery friction and an involuntary muscular spasm some 15 years ago.

This change in relationship is an interesting one. They will now have their own ideas and wills, which will not always be in accord with yours. Indeed, if you're a latecomer to this book and are retrospectively catching up on the contents of this Handbook, your Gangly Lions have probably developed ideas and practices in total opposition to those that you profess. This is called rebellion and has to be handled very carefully, or else you'll both lose, as simple little items escalate into Domestic Thermo-Nuclear War in the bat of a newly mascara'd eyelid. Despite their frequent descent into 'Kevin or Karen Moments', have patience, listen to them, steer them and guide them but be careful not to preach to them. You will find that the infuriating silent insubordination or grumpy response to a simple request is best met by your insistence upon their giving you 'a definite NO'. You can then guarantee their further grumpiness with your own 'definite NO' in return to their next request for a late-night taxi pickup – but you should start to see a change in their responses. From now on, though, the imposition of discipline has got to be based upon respect and logical argument because the "I'm the Daddy and I say so" explanation won't work anymore. Despite your inner urge to swat them as annoying little gnats, you are going to have to meet them intellectually and persuade, cajole and manage your children as you would any junior or employee. After all, you cannot just hand them a P45 and show them the door —you are their lifetime manager in more ways than one.

Family Rules

Of course you will have to have "Family Rules" to set the boundaries around the Protection Principles listed above but they will only work if they are:

Explained – so that the inevitable "Why should I?" retort is pre-emptively destroyed

Fair – because children have an inbuilt sense of fairness that can be easily utilised

Reasonable – so that they are obviously legal, moral and in keeping with the rest of society

Consistently applied – across society and across the family regardless of the age of siblings

Enforceable and Enforced – don't make a law if you can't enforce it and don't make a threat unless you are prepared to carry it out.

The rules that you apply, and the way that you behave, will form the basis for their conscience and you and the rest of Society will reap the rewards of what you sow in the years to come. (Has anybody told the Government this?) If you are gunning for a fight or feel that they are, mentally call a 'Time Out' because you will inevitably go into it hot and bothered and you won't get the result that you really want in the long term. Choose your fights and pick the ones you can win and the ones that you cannot afford to lose, for their sake and safety NOT for your ego and pride. And, if you do get into a bust-up, then have a mutual cooling-off period and find some common ground for a parley later on, once you've remembered that you are the adult as well as the Dad. Help them develop their own sense of responsibility by trusting them more as they get older, especially at the Gangly Lion stage, so that they learn to control themselves through self-discipline rather than imposed discipline. After all, you aren't going to be around them all the time and a quiet whisper and poke in the honesty gland from an inbuilt policeman is a darn sight better than a strong word and an armlock from a real one. Whilst we're discussing legal issues, you can always apply Rule 43 which, under UK law, is a prison regulation whereby offenders can be isolated or segregated for their own protection. The bottom step of the stairs works well for Leg Limpets and 'tweenies but for Gangly Lions you'll need to be a little more abstract: try the interactive/mobile isolation from their peer group - it works the same way if they've always been used to sitting on the 'naughty stair' since they were little.

Whatever methods you apply, it's an interesting challenge and there's lots to learn about them as they develop into adults in their own right — good luck and remember, no matter how bad it gets, you'll only have to go through it once with each one.

Mentors

If you remember back to Chapter 2, we looked at the concept of the Ages of Childhood and the use of a mentor in the third and last phase of childhood.

Choice of mentor - yours or theirs?

"Find a good mentor for your teenagers, before they find a bad one for themselves."

A mentor could be an older brother/sister/cousin, schoolfriend, Godfather/Godmother, father's/mother's friend, neighbour, etc. Remember, you cannot be their mentor, you are their Dad and thus have a totally different relationship and role with your children. At present they will NOT listen to you but they WILL listen to their mentor and therefore if you want to pass them lessons/messages etc, do it through the mentor. If you choose a good mentor, they will observe things about your offspring that you may be able to bring out or help with – dress, manners, general behaviour, language etc. Equally, you might well find that you have to modify your own behaviour and habits in order to influence those of your child. Are you ready for that? Are you willing to put in the effort to change – without taking umbrage or digging yourself an early grave in 'Why Should I?' cemetery? As Gangly Lions, they will naturally rebel, and conflict between parents and offspring often occurs in most cultures.

Activity and Competitive Sport

Apparently, discord is a natural product of the growth spurt, peaking with puberty and declining thereafter. Teenagers see appeasement of their parents, and similar authority models, as subjection contrary to their inner instinct for independence. Their increased competitiveness merely adds fuel to their hostility. In ancient days it was much easier to flex one's youthful muscles because it was a much more physically demanding world. In today's industrial society, youngsters actually have to purposefully set out to be adventurous and independent. Everything that you can do to increase their opportunity for challenge through sport or creativity, or through greater adult responsibility, will help. Conversely, the removal of any sense of natural competition, through a false sense of equal opportunity for all-comers, and the continued selling off of school sports pitches for housing development is likely to hinder their growth and we should fight to bring activity opportunities to our children not take those opportunities away from them. To help cross the 'authority issue' try explaining to your children, and especially your Gangly Lions, that you, Mum and their headmaster and other teachers are here to help them as much as possible.

The Support Team

Try to get them to think of these authority figures as their coaches and training staff, just as in any professional Premier League or National Squads there have to be Directors of Rugby/Football Managers, Head Coaches, Attack and Defence Coaches, Physios, Doctors, Fitness Managers etc). Your family have the role of Home Team Supporters. They are all there to tell them the rules of the game, show them the techniques and short cuts they need to play the game, help them work out the game-plan for each major match and get them match-fit for the Cup Matches. As the Home Team Supporters, the family are there to love and support them, turn up to watch matches, talk to the coaches when they lose or get unfit and, most importantly, cheer them and celebrate when they win. Their job is to get fit, learn and practise the skills they'll need in the matches and give everything they've got in the game, whilst trying not to earn a yellow card and/or ten minutes in the sin bin. They also have to learn though that to stay in the club, they've got to be team players, they've got to go to the training sessions and they've got to put in the effort – otherwise nobody is going to select them for the team, no matter how individually talented they are! They all have individual talents and abilities, but only they can make the best use of them, and only they can play in the matches and score the tries or goals. The rest of us, be we coaches, mentors or just family fans, can only turn up to watch and support them from the touchline.

10
Sex

Rebellion

For those of you who feel depressed, angry, frustrated, ill at ease in the company of others, uncertain about your own sexuality and utterly bewildered by the enigma of the other sex, imagine how your children feel now that they have become 'Gangly Lions'. They have transmogrified into omniscient Masters of the Mobile. Their lives now centre around a small lump of stylish, trilling plastic that rules their universe. It is their lifeline to a social life, acceptability and potential fame - albeit within the limited galaxy of their peer group, and their ability to get through to the Radio One phone-in desk. Any doubts you had about their mathematical abilities may be assuaged by the ease with which they can accurately guage the credit remaining on their Pay as You Go phone card.

Their bodies have out-grown their brain's ability to control them, they feel awkward and unwieldy and their sleep patterns have changed totally so that they will never go to bed in the evening and never get up in the morning. This latter sign of adolescence will be interpreted by you as rebellious laziness, but is actually a result of a hormonal change in cortisol levels. Life will get much easier for you both when you, as the Dad, understand it, accept it and ignore it. (Look up stress and the interesting relationship between cortisol and serotonin. It might help explain why they and you feel like you do during this period). Their language skills will plummet, and they will be transformed from articulate, fluent, little 'tweenies, who never stopped chattering or asking questions, into monosyllabic, grunting apes who only venture into conversation to tell you that you don't understand them personally as people and that the evils of the world are all your fault. This will be an absolute mystery that you will find utterly galling. Whilst abhorrent to you, their choice in music, clothes, hair and new found beliefs are an unconscious initiative to define their own sense of individuality – anything that is different from you will do the trick. If their choice is also likely to infuriate you, then so much the better. So what do you do about them? In short, nothing different to what you have done to date. Keep your temper, stick to your principles and protect your wife and the other domestic Little People. Just reinforce the doorframes and 'password protect' the telephone. For all their newfound bumptiousness they are still your children, wearing your genes as well as your patience and, if you are honest, they are only re-running a classic film of your youth, although it feels more like the 'Addams Family' than 'Little House on the Prairie'.

What they are doing is not new or different

Aristotle wrote about teenagers as: "changeable and fickle in their desires, which are violent while they last, but quickly over: their impulses are keen but not deep-rooted... They cannot bear being slighted and are indignant if they imagine themselves to be unfairly treated." They do not understand the surge of hormones that is coursing through them anymore than you do. But hey, how would you feel if you suddenly woke up and found that you'd gained another solid six inches on your favourite playmate or a pair of pert rounded boobs and curvy hips – you'd be pretty pleased with yourself as well, wouldn't you? They feel as though they are running on high octane aviation fuel, strapped into the cockpit, one hand on the joystick, the other pushing open the throttle and ready to go. You and Mum are the chocks and control tower stopping them from taking off and it doesn't matter to them that you are holding them back until you are sure that the aircraft is serviceable and the wind direction is right. But they are going to take off one day – even if you have to give them a catapult launch, so give them all the flying lessons you can over the next five years. They are going to need them one day. Treat them like potential Aces and, hopefully, they'll turn into aerobats who can elegantly master their flight whilst not losing control of their undercarriage. Your job is to be there at the aerodrome, with a cup of tea (or the fire tender) for when they land.

Sex

The difficult questions are bound to come one day. You and Mum will worry about how you are going to address most of these problems for months before they crash upon you. Yet when they do, it's actually a relief to bring them out into the open. And you can at least make sure that the essential ground is covered. Your Gangly Lions will be far more embarrassed at you bringing up the subject than you are.

In most schools these days, sex education is pretty well taught so most 'twee-nies have a good idea of the physical aspects of it well before they fully under-stand the emotional or social elements. Don't worry about your leg limpets though, they will think that anything to do with willies, bottoms, farts, wee and poo is absolutely hilarious and they are fairly uninterested in the mechanics of it. We suggest that Dads deal with the sons and Mums deal with the daughters – and that you should try to get to them before the actual physical changes come upon them. This is especially important for the girls who need to know that their physical changes are normal, special and nothing to be scared of - or embarrassed about.

Happy and Gay

We are NOT about to pontificate on homosexuality but, if your children decide that they are gay, then remember that whilst it may not be normal (*adj.* 1. conforming to a standard; regular. usual. typical 2. free from mental or emotional disorder (OED)) it is natural (*adj.* 1. existing in or caused by nature 2. in the course of nature; not exceptional or miraculaous (OED)). They will have little to say in whether they want to be homosexual or heterosexual, it appears that you and their mother determined that when they got their initial surges of testosterone and oestrogen at the eight week point in their embryonic formation. They are still your children and still people with individual souls in their own right. Do you think that an omniscient, omnipotent, wholly beneficient God really hates homosexuals? If not, then why should you? It may come as a surprise, but it needn't ruin your or their lives.

Daddy's Little Girl

And talking about daughters, if you hadn't noted it already, remember that a special relationship exists between Daddies and their daughters. Daddy/ daughter relationships are very different to Dad/son relationships. She worships you, just because you are her Daddy, and one day she'll probably bring home the nearest lookalike she can find. But remember that she is not going to be five forever and you are going to wonder where the heck the intervening years went to when you lead her up the aisle to give her to the grinning gorilla at the end of the carpet.

Daddy's Little Girl

Until then, treasure her but don't let her twist you round her little finger. Remind her that you are her Daddy NOT her slave. If in doubt, refer to Mum, who will have great experience of following the same path with her father, and will know most of the tricks that your little darling is about to pull on you. It's a strange thing but, no matter how liberally minded you perceive yourself to be, as a man you will take a sneaking pride in your boys when they start going out with girls but, when some boy starts looking sideways at your daughter, the hairs stand up on the back of your neck and your trigger-finger starts twitching involuntarily. You will instantly experience a temporal wormhole to the memory of yourself as a young teenager, rampant with testosterone and a brand new One-Eyed Trouser Snake with a mind of its own, and you will want to ensure that you don't let one get near your daughter if you can help it. The shocking reality of it is though that

Guidelines for Daddies with Dating Daughters

1) Insist upon meeting her dates, before they take her out. Ensure that you are cleaning your shotguns when they call.....

2) Insist upon the "6 inch rule" in front of you and Mum until at least the third date. Thereafter glancing at her may be allowed so long as it is restricted to her face. Rubbing bumps will result in bumps to rub.

3) Take her date fishing and ensure he sees you gutting a fish – he should begin to understand the meaning of real fear.

4) Insist upon a definite time for return of your most treasured item, in time, in safety and intact. Inform him that 'necking' was a term last used in Paris in 1769 and 'petting' is what people will do to him when he is reincarnated as a poodle in the next life.

5) Insist upon strict manners with your daughter and yourselves. If he respects you enough to be courteous to her while you're there, he might remember enough to respect her when you're not.

6) Ensure that he understands that if she cries, he cries. If in doubt, make him cry at an early stage so that he remembers just before it gets critical.

7) Make sure that he knows that certain places are NOT suitable for dates. These are places where there are beds, sofas, or anything softer than a wooden bench and any place where there are no parents, policemen, or nuns within eyesight. Also places where the ambient temperature is warm enough to induce your daughter to anything more revealing than overalls, a sweater, and a goose down parka zipped up to her throat.

8) Ensure that your daughter shows him your medals, knives and war record. Ensure that you show him your scars and medication.

9) Insist that your daughter's dates meet Mum and if possible her mother as well, so that he has a clear picture of what he is taking on. Make sure that the car has a full tank of fuel – just in case you get a late night call...

10. Wait up for them – and let them know that you will do so.

***"Your daughter IS going to have sex. It's just a matter of where,
when and with whom."***

There are, therefore, some guidelines on dating that are worth following for
your own piece of mind – and that of your daughter, who secretly wants to know
that you still watch over her and care about who she's with.

A reality check

Face up to it, one day you will want your children to have children and to do
that they have got to procreate. Ergo, your children have got to have sex at some
point in time, or else you are not going to be a Grandfather and the family-line
is going to end with them. So, logically, your problem is not IF they have sex, but
when they have sex and with whom they have it. You hope that they will wait
until they are happily married and financially secure enough to be able to cope
with all the additional demands that they placed on you, your wife and your
bank manager. However, that is frankly unrealistic and you probably never did it
so why should you expect them to do so? They are never going to have sex with
you around, or anywhere within the vicinity if they can help it, so in the reality
of a 21st century modern society, the best you could probably hope for is that
they will wait until they are old enough to realise what they are doing and get
the timing right, the person right, the moral basis of it right and ensure that they
don't come to any physical harm. These days, contraception is not just a matter
of making sure that they don't have unwanted pregnancies; there have always
been some fairly nasty sexual diseases around, but with the advent of Aids and
the proliferation of chlamydia and resurgence of syphilis, the practice of safe sex
is becoming not only a preference but a necessity. You can only educate them in
physical safety, moral principles and emotional sense, hope they don't get hurt
too badly or too often and be there to pick up the pieces when they do.

Can I sleep with my boyfriend/girlfriend – in your house?

When the innocent question of sleeping arrangements arises on the impending overnight visit of the girlfriend/boyfriend, don't panic and snap back with an
immediate and provocative "No!" That will only raise hackles and a defiant glare
even though it is your natural instinct and an entirely normal reaction.

Remember that you have a naturally rebellious teenager on your hands and the fastest way of driving them into the arms of another is to offer that as a direct opportunity to rebel against you. Your guiding principles should be those of respect, discretion and sensitivity for the feelings of others. Your children need to understand that they need to respect your territory and home and your rules while you need to understand that they are definitely asking for your support and protection and a re-definition of their position as semi-independent adults. So, remember the logic of the argument above. Sooner or later your offspring ARE going to have sex with someone. You are not going to be there and they are not going to ask your permission beforehand. Therefore, you both need to understand that discretion is the oil to pour on troubled family waters and if you've got the physical, moral and emotional training accomplished properly then you will have little to worry about.

Our guideline, therefore, is that everybody, including visitors, gets their own separate room allocated, to which they retire and in which they should be found as the house awakens. The midnight shuffle that might then occur is discretionary but respect for others within your house is retained and butter still won't melt in her mouth when you meet collectively for breakfast. This might sound like a cop-out or a hypocritical way of dealing with such a situation, but so long as you have taken all the prior steps and got the moral, physical and emotional training right – and as long as they are over the legal age limit, at least you know that they are safe and well. Just make sure that their boyfriends/girlfriends know the ground-rules as well. The same guidelines apply to daughters as well as to sons, but, for the latter, add in the element of a special respect for girls that, hopefully, you will have drilled into them since their earliest days.

The 'kind hands' theory

"The only hands you lay on a girl (or a child) are KIND hands."

For Leg Limpets and 'tweenies, this guideline is more applicable to the physical rule of 'No hitting Girls'. For young male Gangly Lions it's more about additional rules for "Hitting ON Girls" and what their intentions are really set on.

<hr>

Exercise 14:

The Best Contraceptive Going

Find a friend with a 6-9 month old baby. Seek their agreement to co-operate in this exercise. Brief your teenage Gangly Lion that they are going to (literally) babysit the infant for a continuous 24 hour period under the watchful eye of the baby's natural mother. However, they are going to conduct all feeds, nappy changing, walking, activity sessions and maintain all household chores and cook meals for the rest of the family for the day, as if it were their home. Restrict them to the use of one bedroom, kitchen, bathroom and (possibly) one other room. The exercise is suited to both girls and boys. For understanding of the financial implications of a premature family, issue them with their pocket money (to a maximum of £10) and insist that it be used to purchase all nappies, food, mobile phone bills, transport and activities for themselves and the baby for the day. Apply to your local Education Authority to have this exercise included in the National Curriculum for all 13 year olds, repeated on an annual basis.

(Caveat: Do not leave them alone with the baby for a second during the exercise period). If in doubt use a life sized, wee poo cry-a-lot doll.

<hr>

Pornography

The other aspect that you as the Dad will be expected to rule over is the access to, and retention of, pornography. Boys will be boys, and Jessica Rabbit is a darn sight more interesting than Bugs Bunny once the scrotal baggage starts to perform. Your young lions will seek out all and every image of girls that they can. Easy access to a wide range of modern literature and images across the Internet, means that you will need to set clearly defined limits very early on and our guideline is that:

If any image, poster or reading material would offend their mother or sister if she saw it then it's beyond the Pale.

There is some seriously sick and perverted material that can easily be projected at them so a good set of parental control software is essential. You also need sanctions – including the firm understanding that if the family computer or their mobile phone is abused then their access rights will be firmly curtailed for a reasonable period of time. Ensure that they have a secret stash so that Mum doesn't find the discreet pile of Playboy Magazines when she's doing the spring clean. And finally, whilst on matters corporeal, there will come a time, probably when they are Gangly Lions, when sex and deep emotions become mixed up, and relationships get terribly deep. Remember that whether it's Love or Lust, it's just as painful when you fall out of it for the first time. Whilst they may not want you to get involved, and may be too embarrassed to discuss it with you as the Daddy, they will want to know that you are there for them should they want you and your advice. Be there for them, they are going to need you just as much as their Mum, they just haven't found out how to tell you yet – but they'll never forget it if you were there when they needed you.

Educating Daddy

11
'N' drugs 'n' rock 'n' roll

"The only place to get drugs is from a doctor."

Drugs

Drugs are probably one of the greatest threats to the lives of your Little People in the modern world. Alcohol abuse falls well within this category, since it does just as much damage as hard drug abuse, even though it has become so readily available and acceptable within society. Most children want to experiment or are driven to do so in order to appear 'cool' to their peers. As with sex, they are not going to really go for it while you are around, so the best protection you can give them is education and an inbuilt moderator that hopefully kicks in before they do themselves serious damage.

A gradual introduction to alcohol at home is a reasonable way of dispelling the myths of the 'coolness' of drink – their response to their peers can then always be 'Oh, we've had some at home that since I was X years old'. In terms of alcohol, it is always safer to allow a moderation of beer or lager but maintain a firm ruling over spirits. An excess intake of beer or lager will bloat them out before they do too much damage to themselves whilst spirits continue to work on the system even when they are beyond the point of no return and can do serious damage to the adolescent liver and kidneys. Smoking and drugs are somewhat different though.

Smoking is the narrow end of the Dependency Wedge, and can lead to a natural progression to experiment with cannabis smoking and thence (at least theoretically) on the rocky road to tablets, snorting and injections. If you educate them early enough to hate smoking for its smell, fumes and waste products (ash and butts), and a balanced approach to alcoholic drinks you'll save yourself, and them, from a lot of heartache later on. Of course they'll still do the vomiting and hangover phase, but that's what you send them to University for in the first place isn't it? If you're really desperate, try taking them on a boy's weekend to Amsterdam when they are sixteen with a set package of a large Corolla, 15 pints of Amstel, and an hour window-shopping down KanalStrasse. Let Mum know that you are on an educational trip, but in no way let her know the subject matter. Your Gangly Lion will regard you in an entirely different light on the ferry home. Whether you do the same for your daughter depends upon how enlightened you are in your family. (Note: the College Principal, Peter Pater, is eagerly awaiting your subsequent letters and comments on this recommendation).

'n' Rock 'n' roll

Midway through the last century, Rock and Roll was synonymous with the rebellion of youth against the established order. Whilst the musical style was new, the rebellion of the up and coming generation was not; generations of Dads have long questioned and worried about 'the Youth of today' and some new-fangled idea or fashion that their offspring have introduced in order to rebel against the ideals and strictures of 'their elders and betters'. It will seem just the same to you when your Gangly Lions start to stretch their physical and metaphorical limbs as they try to find their own personal independence and style. As with your ideas about their participation in sex,

***And when we were young, your mother was a rib and
I was…er…I was …dust!***

recognize what they are really saying to you and the world in general and what your worries really are in relation to them. Is their statement of long hair, outrageous (or original?) fashion of platform shoes, miniskirts, kaftans or leather jackets really going to destroy the fabric of society as you know and love it? Or are you just rankling at the idea of them being different to you? Does it niggle you that they are not cloned little Mini-Me's? Do you bridle at the thought that they actually dare to have ideas and styles of their own? "Bah! Humbug!" said Scrooge, jealous of their freedom, youthful energy and devil-may-care attitude. All parents have a moment (or five) when they disapprove of their children's friends, fashions or new habits. Remember that it's their life, you cannot live it for them; pulling away from you and finding their own feet is one of the essential tasks of a teenager and part of it is in picking friends, clothes or habits that you loathe. In showing them that you object, you are giving them some-thing to rebel against - in their eyes you are saying that they are not old enough or responsible enough to make their own decisions yet. You can only guide them and apply the same Lifestyle Principles:

Is their new activity or style:

1) Legal? by the laws of the land in which THEY are currently living
2) Physically, mentally or psychologically harmful? (to them not YOU)
3) Morally justifiable? (to the norms of the environment or society in which THEY are living)
4) Financially viable? (to either of you, since you will have to dig them out of the mire)

Unless you get a definite NO to any of these criteria, do as their Mum has always done: smile gently, say "Oh, That's nice dear." and wait. It might be a matter of years, but, they'll come round sooner or later. Indeed, if you show positive approval, the less they will need to rebel - although you might get a few strange looks at work by turning up in Gothic dress with nose, ears, lips and tummy button pierced unless of course you are Ozzy Osbourne.

"If they don't rebel somehow, then how will they test themselves?"

And as for Rock n' Roll and other forms of music, try to keep abreast with what's new and what interests your children. True music has three essential components: rhythm, melody and harmony, but there are an infinitesimal number of ways in which they can be combined to produce 'music' and your Little People's preference is just as valid as yours – even if it is somewhat louder and heavier on the bass element. Do a deal with them so that you listen to their choice if they will listen to yours? When they declare you to be boring, point out how many excerpts of classical music or classic rock and pop are incorporated into popular and current commercials or television programmes that they like. Or you could ask them if they've ever heard of the Beatles, the Rolling Stones, Led Zeppelin or Roxy Music and how old do they think they are at the moment? Truly good music really does stand the Test of Time, so don't worry too much about their current preference for 'Resurrected Transsexual Zombie Rappin' Tossers' because they probably won't be around next year anyway.

12
'N' Booze 'n' cars 'n' bikes 'n' guns

Booze

Alcoholic drink has been a problem for Dads ever since Adam woke to find his fermented berry juice gone and Cain and Abel having a punch-up outside the cave. Drink itself need not be a problem. It tastes nice, it helps you to relax and it appears that there may well be health benefits in wine as well. So you can feel truly self-righteous whilst you enjoy your daily libation at the bar of the gym. You'll probably find that it becomes a problem for you only when your Gangly Lions decide to acquire this 'ornament of adulthood' by exporting the contents of your drinks cabinet out of the back door for consumption behind the bike sheds with other Gangly Lions who also want to appear 'cool'. What used to be just a 'lads' thing has been rapidly expanded to young girls as well with the development of alcopops and a media-driven acceptance of 'ladette' culture as a cool way to behave. It's always fun to see a tantalising flash of knickers, at the top of a shapely thigh – until you realise that it's your daughter who's doing the flashing as she struggles to her feet from the kerbside ditch where she's just parked a curry robed in a six pack of Bacardi Breezers.

"Pickling your liver does NOT make it last longer."

The real problems of drink arise, as with most things, when it is consumed to excess. Try explaining to them that the mild and rather pleasant euphoria, brought on by one or two drinks, rapidly disappears. Make sure that they know that each extra beverage over-inflates both ego and perceived comic ability, increases bravery and aggression (but it slows reactions and decreases fighting ability), reduces physical and mental self-control to eventual catastrophic failure, vastly lowers sexual performance, blurs the vision, mangles the tongue and eventually brings on alcoholic poisoning. Come to think of it, when it's listed like that, it's surprising that a Nanny Government allows anybody to have more than one a day anyway. If you do ever have a meaningful discussion with your own Gangly Lions, then let them know that any fool can look stupid and do silly things, but that they don't have to go binge drinking to do it. They just have to know what the physiological reactions of their own body are to different levels, and mixes, of alcohol. Once they've recognized that, then they and you should-n't have a problem, although it might take them some years before they relate your discussion to the outrageous hangovers they experience. However, since the swine are unlikely to heed your pearls of wisdom until they have experienced it for themselves, the one thing you should insist upon is that they learn the mechanics and reasoning of the Recovery Position so that they, and their friends, don't die of suffocation from their own vomit while unconscious or asleep.

Exercise 15

The Recovery Position

Show your children the Recovery Position and make sure that they know how to put themselves and theirs friends into it. Turn it into a game, so that they can practise it the next time they have a friend over to your house, then at least you'll know they have one Buddy who has the knowledge when they go partying together and you might just have saved another life. If you do NOT know the correct positioning of the body in the Recovery Position, then get a qualified First Aider to show you first. You might also show them the approved method to prevent them from swallowing their tongue.

'n' cars 'n' bikes

It is an offspring's duty to bury its parents and not vice versa, though a youngster's introduction to driving/riding can often lead to a tragic reversal of roles. The hospital medical fraternity are well known for their black humour since it helps them rationalise some of the less palatable aspects of their profession. In the Accident and Emergency wards motor cycle riders and other teenage car-borne Stirling Mosses are colloquially known as either 'Organ Donors' or 'Temporary Citizens'. When your Little People finally take to the road, they automatically arm themselves with a lethal weapon, cunningly disguised as an object of transport. This is fully capable of killing or seriously injuring them and anyone unfortunate enough to be with or near them when they have an accident. It will always be an 'accident', of course. Nobody plans to have a collision otherwise they'd be known as 'deliberates', and it will always be somebody else's fault. There is little you can do about it except to prime them with good driving lessons and a mindset that thinks safety not speed. Don't try to teach them to drive yourself - or they'll drive you to drink. There are far too many arguments, you will worry about your car too much and, if they ever have an accident, you will be the one to blame for your useless instruction. Just do yourself a favour: give yourself an easy life and stand the bill for a qualified instructor. And while we're discussing drinking and driving, make sure they hoist in the Number One Safety Rule:

Never get into a car with a driver who has been drinking

Guns

If you are an English countryman or a traditional American then, in all probability, you'll have your own gun and expect your sons, and possibly daughters, to own their own guns in due course too. There are normally only four reasons for killing anything:

1) It's going to kill you or those you care for.
2) It's seriously wounded.
3) You're going to eat it.
4) It's vermin.

'Looking sideways at me in the bar' does NOT count as a valid reason although it's rather useful to let your daughter's prospective dates know that you own a couple of shotguns as well – one for birds and one for blokes.

Killing for sport is highly questionable in a moral sense unless one is also bound by one of the reasons above – even though as boys, all of us will at some time have taken some perverse pleasure in stamping on an ant/beetle – just because it was there and we could. Such socially psychopathic behaviour is less acceptable once boys progress into adulthood – although nobody seems to have told a significant proportion of a certain Supporter's Club yet.

Education in gun care and use

If you do own and have a license for a gun, an essential responsibility is to educate your offspring in the use and care of guns and other weapons. Primarily, you must ensure that any guns kept in the house are safe, secure and well out of the reach of untrained hands. If you're not sure of what you and they need to know about guns, then question what you are doing with them in the first place and, secondly, get someone who really does know what they are all about to teach you and them. There's no second chances with these issues, so protect them properly first time round.

The Cardinal Rules

"Plan to win the War, not a single battle."

Make sure that you, and they, focus on the really important rules. The Cardinal Rules for the modern world, so far as they relate to your Little People, are those issues that are most likely to keep them out of serious trouble or stop them from damaging their lives irrevocably. They are underpinned by 'Mutual Trust and Understanding', which will be a foundation for all of their relationships, not just the one they have with you and their Mother. They need to be spelt out clearly and with the full explanation that they are for their safety and wellbeing, not just because you are a boring old git who has never been a cool dude. But Little People need to have easily available hooks upon which to hang the important things that they'll need later in life – so we have the 'the big five', one important rule for each finger on the hand that says STOP:

1) **Don't Drink and Drive**
2) **Don't do Drugs**
3) **Do Safe Sex**
4) **Do keep a Secret**
5) **Do Respect your Mate** (and his/her Money, Beer, and Bird/Bloke)

If they can follow that code, be they sons or daughters, then they have a good chance of making it through to adulthood with their honour, their friends and a healthy mind, body and soul.

Homework:

During the next week:

1. Plan a specific time to chat with your children about 'the Big Five'.
2. Sex (depending on age of your child). Check out what they know and what they ought to know (Check it out with Mum first – don't tackle it on your own). It's a BIG hurdle (at first) but if you explain your worries about them (Physical, Moral, Emotional –Financial) and their welfare as the first hop, you (and they) should be OK with it.
3. Drugs – discuss who takes drugs that they know....(someone will be doing so). Find out what's available - and what they've tried or what they are tempted to try.
4. Music – listen to a record of their choice with them. (Bonus mark if you can get them to listen to a classical record with you)
5. Go through the current Top Ten Chart with them, with a (brief) listen to each record and find out which ones they like and why. (Bonus mark if you make it the whole way)
6. Offer your Gangly Lion an alcoholic drink, in a reasonable measure, and take them through the distinction between Grain and Grape and the benefits of NOT mixing the two.
7. If you own a gun, book them a coaching course at your local shooting school or fix up a lesson with a local gamekeeper. You might also book a visit to a conservation site at the same time.
8. Organize a 'Family Film Night with a Difference', and incorporate...
A film about Aids or other STDs.
A film about drug abuse and its related effects.
A film about organ donors and/or road traffic accidents.
A film about Drinking and Driving.
A film about Gunshot wounds.

Educating Daddy

Part Four - Family Matters

Or why Dads need a shed

Educating Daddy

Family Matters
Why Dads need a shed

This final part of Educating Daddy deals with those issues that you are likely to come across whether your offspring are Leg Limpets, 'tweenies or Gangly Lions and, because of the nature of the material, it is rather more reflective, laden with gravitas and, at times, downright critical of current social and political practice. At this point in the book, we are dealing with 'Issues'; the Oxford English Dictionary definition of 'Issue' is sixfold, all of which are applicable at one time or another when considering family and fatherhood:

1. Giving out or circulation of shares, notes or stamps.
2. An outgoing or outflow.
3. A point in question, an important subject of discussion or litigation.
4. A result or outcome.
5. Children , progeny.
6. A discharge of blood.

Hence:

Issue(s) Issue(s) Issue(s)

There are many things that your Little Ones are going to spring upon you in the years to come. Not all of them will be welcome, timely or cheap. However, when it all does go wrong, in the heat of the moment keep two things focussed firmly in your mind: 'Have I done the best thing to support and develop my child?' and, 'When I look back on this in ten years time, did I deal with it so that the long term effects achieved what I really want for young Herbert / Gertrude?' The same question may also be asked of your wife/ partner, so read the chapter on SHE who must be obeyed very carefully…because SHE will, and SHE'll notice if you don't apply it.

This final part also contains some interesting thoughts on the Application of Fatherhood Theory to Business and Management just so that you can get your company / boss to send you on a seminar that will allow you to discuss all of this and pay you to do it as well. Now there's an offer your wife won't refuse!

Having plumbed the depths of what might go wrong or is difficult in your paternal life, take Hope for there is also light at the end of the tunnel, you might graduate soon if you have been following the Course in this book, and there are rewards for good boys too….

Educating Daddy

13
When Things go Wrong

Law Enforcement

It's all a matter of trust. You will be expected to keep your word, as a matter of honour. Both your Little People and their Mum will know if you don't and they will remind you of it often. This is applicable to both threats and promises. If you set rules for your Little People with a running scale of penalties for breaking them, you have to be both ready and able to enforce them. If you don't, then don't expect them to respect your 'word of law' at all next time. Obviously, your punishments need to be in proportion to the crime, or else you will not be able to apply them, the threat will not be credible, and you won't be believed. Under the terms of the Geneva Convention, you cannot use the removal of food, clothing, shelter or first aid in any form, sleep deprivation should only be practised by them not you and torture is definitely frowned upon by the Social Services. Remember also that digital amputation can only be used as an effective deterrent nine times and then you'll both have problems when you ask them to fetch anything for you in future. Respect for you, Mum and your collective system of values is really the key and it will become more apparent as your Little People become too big to handle. Just wait and see.

"Don't make a threat unless you are capable of fulfilling it."

Keeping Your Word

There are two types of promises: stated and implied. If you say to a Little Person that you will do something then they will hope that you do so – and they might get upset if you don't. But, if you Promise to do something for a Little Person, then they will expect you to do so and will get upset if you don't.

The statement that you will try to do something has an Implied Promise, and you have some leeway for escape if you forget or if you cannot do what you have said you'll try to do. With the Stated Promise, however, you have no leeway at all and both the Little People and Mum WILL turn the handle on the testicular vice if you don't deliver. This may seem to be a blinding glimpse of the obvious, but it is too easy to underestimate the store that little minds set on promises and their fulfilment. They will trust you implicitly to never break a promise and only you can teach them otherwise through the experiences that you put them through. The corollary of course is that you will expect them to keep their promises to you and to others. But if they haven't been taught that you will keep your word, then how can you expect them to keep theirs?

"You are expected to keep your promises, and so are they."

Physical Violence

One day in a moment of exasperation, primeval instinct will take over and the flea-bitten old warrior lion will snarl at his cubs and take a swipe at a leg or backside with a hefty paw. Realising how close it came to sudden and violent death, the cub will whimper off to the lioness who, as the provider of comfort and protection, will lick its wounds and pick her time to chew the ass off the Pride of the Pride. Smacking, shaking and other forms of Actual Bodily Harm (ABH) have certain major effects: in the short term, you release pent-up frustration through physical action and your offspring submit to your immediate will; in the long term, you feel utterly dissatisfied with your handling of the situation and your Little People feel resentment at having been physically abused by one who is meant to be a comforter and protector. It is interesting to note that Mums and Dads are more likely to smack if they are an unsupported partner than if they have no partner at all, so an agreed collective policy and recognized scale of punishment and reward that is practised consistently across the family will do more for them and you than a poorly timed whack across the back of the head.

"Smacking is NOT an effective long term deterrent."

Although it sounds namby-pamby, pinko-trendy, and fashionably 'Politically Correct', the School of Reasoned Logic really is a more effective way of training future grown-ups. There is a whole gamut of sanctions that can be imposed before resorting to rearranging your children's facial features. Try removal of television, Playstation, mobile phone, and limited access to cigarettes and whisky first. And be firm about it.

Setting the Boundaries

Children actually appreciate knowing where the boundaries are placed although they will keep bouncing off the wire to see how far they can explore. Just make sure that you are consistent about where you have set the fence-line and confident about your right to teach them what is right and wrong. As they grow and learn, it is part of your job as a Dad to move the fence-line back so that they can explore a little further each time. It is up to you to measure how far and how freely you will let them roam. You will find, however, that they will occasionally burrow under whatever fence-line you have set, like little rabbits trying to get at the juicy carrots beyond. So, like good gardeners, you just have to keep watching for the rabbit runs and blocking the holes as you find them. Things will go wrong, dummies will get spat out and teddies will get thrown out of the pram. The real issue is what you do about it when it happens. If you are slow off the mark then they will either get into serious trouble or injure themselves. Alternatively you'll find that they got in their excuse early, 'turned Mummy's Evidence' and got off lightly with a hug while you copped a Zero Tolerance sentence and ended up in serious poo with SHE who must be obeyed.

The real secret of dealing with your children is to change the tone of your voice to reflect how and what you want them to listen to. If you act like a boxing manager, screaming terse instructions that brook no argument then don't be surprised if they switch off after the first round. Instead, make sure that they look you in the eye, and keep your words to a few well thought out, steady and firm instructions. You are much more likely to get a positive response. Whatever it is you want to tell them, think: slow and steady, relaxed and patient. Throw a strop and you've lost them. If it all becomes too hot and noisy, let it cool down and then find common ground for a parlay. Just remember to retain realistic expectations and remember that things aren't always black and white. Though you might like to create cloned Mini-Me's, your offspring have minds, wills and thoughts of their own. These are necessarily different to yours. Allow them the freedom to think, just help them to shape their thoughts for a positive purpose.

The Civilized World works through diplomacy, persuasion, and a balance of threat and promise in an effort to improve the lot of the whole. The Uncivilized

World, by contrast, resorts to violence and disorder in an effort to improve the lot of the individual. Their world will reflect the one that you choose to introduce to them. So choose your fights carefully; pick the ones that you can win and, especially, the ones that you cannot afford to lose.

Exercise 15

The Penal System

Fill in the table below based upon what happened to you, your parents and what you would like to see happen to your children. Every punishment should have an element of Retribution, Recompense and Deterrence: talk to your partner about the scale of punishments you could apply to your own children and under what circumstances.

PUNISHMENT	PARENTS	YOU	CHILDREN
Explain/Discuss	Unlikely	Probably	Likely
Forced formal apology	Probably	Unlikely	Unlikely
Forced written apology	Possibly	Unlikely	Unlikely
Sent to room/isolated	Probably	Probably	Probably
Smack	Likely	Probably	Possibly
Removal of toys/games	Likely	Likely	Probably
Gating	Possibly	Possibly	Possibly
Restriction of Privileges	Unlikely	Possibly	No mobile/internet)
Caning or Beating	Probably	Possibly	Unlikely
Police Involvement	cuff round the ear	informal warning	formal caution/ASBO
Formal Execution	Only for murder	Divorce instead	Deportation to Slough

Hint: We have filled in the table as a starting point for discussion within your family on the basis of current trends of social behaviour in UK. It is of course up to you whether you decide to deport the children to Slough earlier in the disciplinary process. If you are already resident in Slough, we offer our heartfelt commiserations, hope your parole comes up soon and wish you all the best with your cabbages (viz: Sir John Betjeman).

Useful Behavioural Guidelines

1) Try to give no offence to other people
2) Fight only to defend and protect - not to take what is not rightfully yours
3) Limit your physical action to what is necessary – not to what you are capable of doing
4) Do not wilfully damage property and be prepared to make good any damage that you do
5) Do to others as you would have done unto you

It goes without saying that lying, cheating and stealing are distinctly frowned upon and rape, murder and coveting your neighbour's wife or goat are definitely OUT. It's amazing how many modern Dads have forgotten some of these things – try not to be one of them.

Saying Oops! & Sorry

One of the most important lessons for Little People is to learn how to say sorry. We all offend one another, tread on someone else's toes or borrow something and forget to return it sooner rather than later. If you do not fit into any of these categories then a stained glass window in York Minster is yours for the asking. For the rest of us, the eating of measured portions of Humble Pie, with sprinklings of Regret and a dollop of Shame Custard has to be forced upon us.

"You CAN apologise to your children and it doesn't hurt."

A Little Person will rarely go and apologise without direction from you or Mum. If they don't learn the importance of it early on, then they'll never learn to apply the lesson later on. Again, it's back to you as a Dad, with essential input from Mum, to make sure that they know the score. If they don't apologise of their own accord, they'll be dragged round by the earlobes to do so in front of you. Which one is less embarrassing?

Anger and Self-Control

Most anger arises because you get yourself into a situation that you cannot control or because you fear that someone or something you care about may get damaged. Prolonged stress shortens the fuse and the likelihood of an early explosion rises. However, Little People, and even Gangly Lions, are not good at recognizing stress in their Mums and Dads and therefore don't know how or why to pull back. It's up to you to prepare yourself before you come back into contact with your Little People. They will NOT understand why you are short-tempered, feeling unloved, worried for them/about them/because of them.

Understand that all they want is some of your total attention. Even if you give them only 15 minutes of total absorption per day, they will be satisfied. If not, then you and they will start getting into the realms of Attention Deficit Syndromes and the multiple complications that follow on from there. So, if you regard it as a business proposition, it's cheaper, easier and ultimately more rewarding to invest in the time and energy early on.

Equally, when you do give them your 15 minutes of undiluted attention, try to make it an occasion for Praise, Praise, Praise not Criticise, Criticise, Criticise. It is all too easy for Daddy to be seen as the person who inflicts rules and regulations of the House rather than someone who is pleased that his Little People have made progress towards achieving their goals. You can build or damage self-esteem in your youngsters so easily that you will have to make a conscious and deliberate decision to be measured in your criticism and free with your praise. Recognize that they, like you, respond much better to a smile and an approving comment than they do to grumpy scowls and yet another bout of parental recrimination.

When they next come into the room you're in, make a positive, conscious effort to look at them with love in your eyes and a smile rather than with a Judge's appraising glare, ready for conviction and sentence. This is not just a glib remark or a fashionably 'clever' thing to do, it actually works and it actively changes the way that you act/react to your children. Remember that all children are different and that they all develop at different rates. It is easy to 'judge' them too quickly whilst forgetting that they need time to grow and develop and you may need to temporarily lower your hurdles so that they can clear them.

Just to make you keep your feet on the ground, take a look at this letter home from Charlotte to her father…..

Dear Daddy,

I am writing this from hospital where I was taken last night, after my boyfriend crashed your car. You haven't met him yet but he is a really nice Bosnian Serb and whilst he hasn't got a proper UK license yet, he normally drives pretty well. I have broken my pelvis - he is pretty smashed up too. He failed the breathalyser and the Police found some cocaine in the car and are about to interview us.

To make matters worse, the hospital blood test revealed that my boyfriend has Aids - and they have just told me that the blood test also shows I am pregnant too.

Daddy, I'm frightened, please come and visit me - sorry about all this.

Lots of Love

Charlotte

PTO

147

Actually, none of this is true, but I have just
failed my first year exams and I thought that
this might help you to keep things in
perspective!

Love

Charlotte
xxx

It's all about managing expectations!

Apologies

At some point in time, you are going to offend your own Little People AND their Mum. Try not to let it happen simultaneously or else apologies have to be accompanied by flowers, chocolates and at least a week's penile servitude (sic). Your Little People come with an inbuilt Fairness Barometer, which has been

Exercise 16

Ten Steps to Heaven

There is an ancient, anonymous, Judeo-Christian decalogue that is worth getting your Little People to remember by rote. Even if you profess total atheism, adherence to most of the Christian ideals can do little harm, and may do a great deal of good. Adherence to the ten commandments does make for a quiet life and the fifth line of this homily is a definite must for teenagers.

Thou, no God shalt have but Me,
Before no idol bend thy knee;
Take not the name of God in vain,
Nor dare the Sabbath day profane;
Give both thy parents honour due,
Take heed that thou no murder do;
Abstain from words and deeds unclean,
Nor steal, though thou be poor and mean;
Nor make a wilful lie, nor love it,
What is thy neighbour's, do not covet.

"And for not eating all your vegetables, you shall be taken from this court to a place of lawful execution......"

149

tuned by you, but which also measures your own performance against the standards that you set them. If you make a mistake in your handling of them or show favouritism, they will pounce on it quicker than ferrets on a fluffy bunny. You will take the title role of Bobtail. You will NOT feel like apologising to your own children at all but, like drinking childhood cough medicine, even though you don't like doing it, it will make you feel better afterwards and it'll get easier next time. Just don't make a habit of it.

Forgiveness

One of the greatest attributes of a Father is to dispense forgiveness. We all go wrong occasionally, we all offend each other, we all try to live in a world full of friction where selfishness rather than selflessness predominates. Forgiveness is a necessary part of living in a community and, whilst saying sorry is an important part of growing up, so too is the art of forgiving - and meaning it! Too many people say "it's OK" or "forget it" and then harbour a grudge. If something rankles after an incident or offence, then talk it out until it no longer hurts, chafes or offends. This is a most neglected area in many people's social education and your Little People will only learn it from you and through the way that you explain it to them. So, if they offend you or their peers, you have to show them how to ask for forgiveness.

Count the Cost

Equally, if they are hurt or offended against, they must learn how to forgive with a free heart and not 'Count the Cost'. A warning though, it's very difficult to do because, unless you were taught this yourself when you were a Little Person, you'll be fighting decades of righteous indignation and personal tallies of who 'owes' you. Now that it's been pointed out to you, you'll notice how you have inadvertently injected 'Count the Cost' into your daily life already – how many times do you say: "I've just put the bins out **for you**", or "I've just fed the cat **for you**?" SHE has noticed for some time now, and still hates it. Do yourself a favour, rip up the scorecard and give the World a second chance. It will change your life. Practise this with Mum and you'll have a very settled marriage and home. This will also make it doubly easy to teach the Little People.

"It's OK to ask for help."

While we're on the subject of getting it wrong and putting it right, just remember that you are not alone and it has been done before by billions of men before you. Some got it wrong and their children paid the price for it. Most got it right, however, and as a result we have a wonderful world to thank them for. If in doubt as to how you are doing, look at your children and remember what you want them to be – then ask yourself what you have to do to match the two visions.

There is always help around if you need it, either informally through other parents, your own extended family or, if it's really bad, then through official organisations. You can hire a Nanny, Au Pair or at the other end of the scale, you can call in a Social Worker. However, none of the help that you can get, can fully replace you and the very special time, attention and relationship with your Little People that is yours, and theirs, by right.

If things go badly wrong, retreat to your shed. Every Dad needs a shed where he can be on his own. Men internalise and women externalise when it comes to problem solving. Men, and thus Dads, need to think out a problem whilst Women, and thus Mums, need to talk out a problem. Dads therefore need somewhere to think, hum, sulk, plan, pray and gain respite. Hence, the need for Dad's Shed. This truth has been around for a long time and archaeologists in Africa have even found a side-cave that Adam used filled with spare bits of rib, assorted flintheads, and wall paintings of snakes, apples and naked Eves.

Happiness

The following exercise is intended to allow you to help your children face the world around them with confidence and a happy smile. We all naturally tend to think well of people who smile at us, it relaxes us, makes us feel less vulnerable and leaves us in a happier memory of that person. This exercise is especially useful for your Gangly Lions, who have metamorphosed from the carefree, smiling angels you used to tuck into beddie-byes with Teddy and a snugly kiss, into grunting, morose, awkward creatures, who are too shy to look you confidently in the eye (never mind a real stranger or a member of the opposite

The Ode to a Garden Shed

Robbie "Ploughboy" Burns, the renowned Scottish Poet, who fathered a dozen children, knew a thing or two about the Dad's need for sanctuary, and he eulogised his own sacred hideyhole in one of his less well-known poems:

Here's tae ye, wee auld wooden shed,
Mae garden haeme an' sanctr'ry,
In ye I hide an' shaeke mae hed,
At women's ways an' fancies.

Nay bairns or babbies ye'll find in here
There's far tae many dangers
Frae blades or ropes an' bits o' gear
Fer Young Divills with wee fingers

Ah'm safe inside yer rick'ty walls
From skirts – most always sassy,
Men Only 'llowed – Flat chest, Two Balls,
Which rules out any lassie

Aye – safe awa from waspish tongues
Where ma candle dimly flickers
Ah'll dream of beer, n' cars, n' guns
And anything in knickers.

So here's tae ye, mae faithful shed
Fie ev'ry day that passes,
A toast for all the hours spent
In you - and all those lassies.

sex) and whose favourite expression appears to be a scowling grimace. Your 'tweenies will love the idea and competitiveness of the game and your leg limpets will practise it naturally with no trouble whatsoever.

And finally, whilst we dwell on what to do when things go wrong, remember that things do go right as well and giving them a pat on the head works wonders for them and you. That may sound fatuous but it's too easy to forget that, whilst we are trying desperately to turn our children into honest, kind, stable and productive members of future society we also need to ensure that they are truly happy. Indeed establishing their long-term happiness and equipping them with the tools to maintain it should probably be our focus anyway. Happy children, typically, have a secure and loving relationship with their parents, generally get on well with other children and have one or two really good friends. Conversely, unhappy children are withdrawn, find communication difficult, and tend towards the insular and insolent.

Exercise 17

Make 'em Smile.

The idea of the game is to make other people smile. The count starts anew at the beginning of each day and the winner is the person with the highest total by the end of the day. Positive counts are gained by making people smile before they make you smile and, conversely, negative counts are debited if they smile at you before you smile at them, or if you do not return their smile. Once you or they have smiled you cannot target them for a second score. The art therefore is to get them before they get you. Obviously, you can expand this game/exercise to incorporate strategies to play a competitive game between siblings. Try it yourself, it's good fun and looking like a total looney to perfect strangers in a crowded street is all part of the game. You will soon notice that you will slip into practising this game unconsciously and will inwardly curse when someone scores off you rather than your scoring off them. There's only one way to win, and that is to proactively smile all day. Other side effects are that people will notice your 'sunnier' disposition, your personal relations will change and your inner confidence will grow. Imagine the effect on an awkward teenager. Now play the game....

Emotional Intelligence

The foundation of happiness is esteem for oneself and for the rights and dignity of others. Such esteem is born out of the establishment and maintenance of personal and social relationships. The key factor here is ensuring that your child has good Emotional Intelligence (EI). Emotional Intelligence, like any other form of standardised Mensa-style intelligence is a product of both nature and nurture. We are all born with an innate level of EI but can also be educated to a higher level by those who care for us. By doing so we can reach a level of social competence that will enable us not only to survive in the world, but to prosper in it as well. EI education is concerned with teaching how to recognize feelings and responses in other people, how to work out whether someone is sad or angry, jealous or afraid and, more importantly, how to respond to them. Equally important is the need to recognize the same emotions within oneself. We must also learn to control our feelings if we are to manage a situation and ensure the best outcome for everybody. Valuable EI life-skills are: understanding motivation and recognizing 'cause and effect', verbal and written communication skills and, importantly, a correct use of humour – the saviour of any situation. The outcome of good EI education should be an individual who is equipped to recognize a situation, understand their part in it, make a value-based judgement and then act upon it. Too often these days, young people accomplish the first and last parts of the equation without performing the middle two sections as well and then wonder why it all went wrong. The inevitable result? Unhappiness.

The OODA Loop

An invaluable decision making process – commonly applied in business and useful to the Dad, resulted from one young fighter pilot's experiences during the Korean War, and by his subsequent analysis of air combat in Vietnam. Colonel John Boyd (known as '40 second Boyd' for the remarkable speed with which he despatched enemy fighters) worked out that combat success was based on making good decisions quicker than your opponent. Boyd's input shaped the Lockheed Martin F-16 – the most agile and most successful fighter of its generation. The aircraft has a massive bubble canopy giving its pilots an almost unequalled and unobstructed view of the outside world, allowing them to acquire their targets earlier in the topsy-turvy tumble of dogfights, and therefore gaining extra seconds deciding how to react and manoeuvre into a position to open fire effectively. The key, however, was the theory of the 'OODA' loop upon which the cockpit design was based.

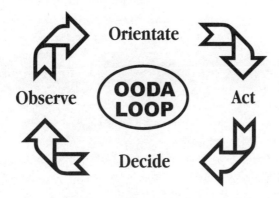

The OODA loop recognizes the critical relationship between Observation, Orientation, Decision and Action and its feedback into an ongoing situation. The important thing to note of course is that if an individual, or an organisation, can establish a tight OODA cycle then it can make decisions and react to any given situation quicker and more effectively than others in the same environment. This theory has become one of the essential bases of progressive military thinking in the late 20th Century, which has infiltrated into business strategy and, rightfully, should now progress into personal relationship and childcare practice. If we can educate our children to consciously Observe, Orientate, Decide and then Act, we have a chance that they will not only think about what they are doing but also take note of the reaction it creates and respond accordingly. This should in turn create young individuals who are truly empowered to make their own decisions and take responsibility for their own lives thereby making them, and us Dads, happier in the process. Interestingly, neither EI nor OODA is taught in schools although it could (should?) be included in the Citizenship modules that are the mode to insert into the National Curriculum at present. Next time you see a group of teenagers hanging around on a street corner, try to work out if their total EI quotient is over 10 or not: if it's under 10, engage your own OODA loop, cross the road and ring the Education Secretary's Hotline.

Educating Daddy

Homework

During the next week.....

1) Make a list of all the people that you consider have hurt you, done you down, offended you, insulted you, gone behind your back ...get the idea? Now get a punch-bag and a pair of 16-ounce gloves. One at a time, pin a photo or cartoon of the target above your punch area and focus your anger on each person as you take it out on the punch-bag. Concentrate solely on your hurt and resentment. Then wipe the slate clean and move on.

2) Make a list of all the people whom you may have hurt, done down, offended, insulted, gone behind their back.....Who me? Now get a punch-bag and a pair of 16-ounce gloves. Ring them up and ask them if they'd like to meet you at the Gym. Stand in front of the punchbag ..... Still feel so self-righteous?

3) Count how many times you have smacked your children. If you need to take off your shoes and socks to assist in the tally, then seek counselling – and not just for remedial maths.

4) Create a 'Count the Cost' card for yourself and Mum. Score what you do over the next week and then compare cards. You will then want to burn cards, buy her flowers and promise her 30 minutes of concentrated oral pleasure if she promises not to tell her girlfriends about it and an hour if she forgets the sorry incident altogether.

5) Go online and Google an Emotional Intelligence Quotient quiz. Do the quiz. If you get less than average, look up Emotional Intelligence and How to Improve your Score: (a hint: spend less time on the computer and more face to face time with your family).

14
SHE (Who Must Be Obeyed)

For two thousand endless years, Ayesha (She) who maintained her vigil with supernal powers that could have made emperors her slaves, was the omnipotent Witch Queen of the debased and savage Amahagger. This awesome beauty represented power, passion and beauty as well fireside, home, family, and most importantly... love... All in one woman! (From the classic novel 'SHE' by Sir Henry Rider Haggard).

The reality of the Domestic Goddess

Let's get things in their proper perspective here. The difference between a wife and a girlfriend is about 45 pounds and the difference between a husband and a boyfriend is about 45 minutes. Do not expect her to be dressed in fishnets and French Maid's outfit when you walk in the door. Where once YOU were *Numero Uno, Le Grand Fromage sur L'Assiette de La Femme, Der FliegermausHerren* to her *KatzeFrau*, you have now been supplanted by aliens of your own making and you are no longer the Centre of Her Universe.

What you hoped for...

What you get!

Dad's real place in the order of priorities

Of necessity, Mums are schizophrenic Sex Goddess/Housekeepers* and, usurped by Little People, you are now shooting down the Family Priority order as rapidly as you can produce more offspring. If you are really unlucky then you'll average out at Number 9 in the Maternal Pecking Order behind:

(1) Your youngest child
(2) Your oldest son
(3) Your daughter
(4) Her mother
(5) Her father,
(6) Her favourite brother/sister
(7) Her dog/cat and
(8) her ski/tennis coach.

It's not that SHE doesn't love you anymore, it's just that SHE has become a Mummy and now she has to concentrate on them because they need her more than you do.

> *"SHE does still love you and she'll let you know once the children are in bed. If you're lucky."*

Keep cool, stud. You'll get your chance after the 9 o'clock watershed, and so long as you've applied the lessons in Chapter 3 about sharing the load, you'll have made your bed and she'll lie in it with you. On the other hand, if you've comprehensively blown it and if SHE really has put you down at Number 9, get yourself an 'Oh! Pere' and console yourself with the few thoughts opposite, Translated from the poem 'What's on a Man's Mind?' by Sigmut Foxley-Freud:

Time Out

They always say that 'familiarity breeds contempt' whilst 'absence makes the heart grow fonder' and it's true. Both Mums and Dads need space, from each other <u>and</u> from the Little People. If it doesn't occur through the natural routine

What's on a Man's Mind

When thoughts of girls pervade male minds,
(Men know me not a Liar),
They tend towards the lowest kinds,
Though some might wish them higher.

For dainty foot and pretty shoe,
May lead to 'Male Brain Stoppage'
Whilst eyes are cast down well below
The mind plays 'Hide the Sausage'.

That shapely ankle 'pon the stair
Whose curve he'd yearn to cup,
Gives rise to thoughts of sweeter fare
'Bout two feet further up:

A well-turned calf in silken hose
Can cause Man's head to pound,
Though gaze is fixed from knees to toes
His heart's set on 'Love's Mound'.

Upon that rounded knee he'd place
A hand, and hope to melt
Resistance in the ancient race
To skin the Beaver of her pelt.

Along those curving thighs he'd run
His mind, in pursuit of the Hunt
Which fires his imagination
To conjure a more cunning stunt:

O Men, you'll find there is no doubt
Your fortune lies upon Her whim.
Tho't took nine months to pop you out
Your life's true quest's to slip back in!

Caveat for all Mums, Grandmas etc who might be reading this Handbook: the inclusion of this section is for HIM not you. Do not bother getting overly-prudish or incensed by what's really on HIS mind, just make sure that YOU remain the focus of it.

of modern life, then it has to be purposefully manufactured into the rhythm of the family. Occasionally, SHE wants to be able to put the children to bed and slob around in Winceyette and slippers on the settee with a couple of girlfriends drinking white wine, eating pizza and watching weepie movies. But don't ruin your marriage by watching it. Do yourself and her a favour by going away for a couple of nights with the Boys and let her get on with it. If you plan it correctly, you can take the older Gangly Lions camping, or on some other 'Boys Trip' and earn double the Bonus Marks whilst having good fun – if you want to go the whole hog, you can bond and hug each other as well.

It's worth also sending her away once in a while, but the deal is different here. Your job as the Dad -Person is then to replace Mum for a few hours/days and allow her to get her balance and sanity back. Remember that it is only for a finite time and SHE should come back. SHE must leave you a timed and detailed list of what to do for each Limpet and you'll need an Emergency Contact List of her other Mummy girlfriends who will know what to do when the proverbial poo goes airborne. She will return to you, happy, calm, refreshed and pleasantly amazed that you are all still alive. You will need a rest at the office.

Is there sex after children?

If you are a new Dad, the sneaking worry in the front, middle and back of your Freudian head is whether there is going to be any sex at all once SHE has had the first child. Of course there is Silly, but when, how often and where is dependent on a whole gamut of factors that you'll both experience. Sex will depend on mental and physical exhaustion, her physical condition, her psychological condition and possible depression, your ever-decreasing bank balance, your conflicting demands of job and home, and the seemingly incessant demands of the new alien. Even if you do still get the urge, most of these pressures are more likely to send Sergeant Sausage off to Floppyland than onto Guard Duty at the Palace of Love.

However, rest assured, the day will arrive when SHE produces both her GP's 'fit to fly' certificate and the will to get back into the cockpit. Your best aphrodisiac is the one between you ears not the one between you legs, so use it to prepare yourselves mentally for this eventuality by employing one or two good bonking strategies:

1) 'The Quickie': Spontaneity will offer you the chance of a quick snatch of relief. The almost illicit 'naughtiness' of it will bring a piquancy to the experience as you try to squeeze one in before the little Herbert wakes – or the Health Visitor arrives.

2) 'The Slowie': Plan for the moment. Arrange a diary date with your wife. OK, so it's less passionate that the Quickie but it's a darn sight less tense, so long as you've taken the phone off the hook, put the dogs in the kitchen, told her mother you're away for the day and have parked the car round the block. Try suggesting a game of "Whose Zoo?" which starts with the opening line: "You bring Pussy and the Puppies and I'll bring Python and the Rabbit!"

As you gain more and more children, the demands of domestic life will pull you and her in a number of different directions and if you still hanker after the Sex Goddess then you just have to set it up for yourself. Make no mistake here, we're NOT advocating adultery. But if you want to sneak Desmond the Dalek into the Velvet Tardis to transport the pair of you off to another planet then you're going to have to take Mum well away from her current orbit where she feels constrained by the cries and crises of Little People. Only then will she return to being the Saucy Little Minx who seduced you in the first place.

The Minx is still in there and desperate for a chance to get out every once in a while. However, you have to let her out by fixing up a highly trusted weekend child-sitter and investing in a Country House Hotel room at least 50 miles away. SHE will take care of the rest, just give her the chance to adjust her mind and libido to take full advantage of the opportunity.

"The odds are against both you and SHE being psychic you have to remember to keep communicating."

Family Calendar

We recommend that you keep a family calendar with a column for each family member. This enables you to know where you are meant to be and thereby avoid disappointment and total global thermonuclear war. As a Dad, you now have to think and organise as part of a family group.

Exercise18

Family Planning Diary

This has nothing to do with condoms or trying to sort out the best day in the oestrogen cycle to get pregnant. Let us work out how good you are at family planning by co-ordinating diaries and events. This will allow you to determine how far you have to go in order to take a more active role in family life and stop you getting the domestic crap kicked out of you for missing important family activities:

January: It is New Year's Day. You wake with the Mother in Law of all hangovers (it's a real cow) only to find that the children want to go sledging, your wife wants to go to the Sales and you just want to die peacefully in your bed. Do you:
a) Turn over and go back to sleep until the world stops spinning.
b) Say "OK, Kids, let's hit the slopes and let Mum hit the shops. Here, Darling take Mr Plastic with you and enjoy yourself, I put £10,000 into the current account for this day!"
c) Book the family on a flight to Switzerland and a 4 man Bob down the Cresta Run: 'You want sledging? I'll give you sledging....'

February: You have been invited to the wedding of a luscious old 'squeeze' from your bachelor days in London. On consulting the diary you find that it conflicts with your 'tweenie daughter's Pony Club Rally and your Gangly Lion's Valentine's Day party, so you:
a) Get tickets to the Lion King for your wife and the children and go to the wedding party yourself.
b) RSVP "yes", book a 5* hotel and book grandparents for the kids and the full body treatment for your wife so that she feels like £1,000,000 on the day and you get your money's worth for a night without the kids.
c) Hire out your daughter's pony as novelty entertainment for the Reception, slip a bridesmaid £20 to chat up your teenage son and give your Leg Limpet free access to the Film Channel and mini-bar in the hotel room.

March: You have been invited to an all expenses paid Business Hospitality Day at the Six Nations Rugby Final between England and France in Paris. You have forgotten that it is your Wedding Anniversary. Do you :
a) Explain that it is a key business meeting on which a vital contract and therefore your promotion to Senior Executive rests. Get your secretary to send HER flowers on the business account.

b) Take your wife anyway. She can shop while you go to the match and meet up for dinner in Mont Martre afterwards.

c) Engineer a family crisis between HER parents which needs her immediate presence. Adopt puppy dog eyes as you see her off at the station. Give the kids £20 for food for the weekend and catch the next Eurostar.

April: Your wife signed you up to run the Easter Egg Hunt for the Leg Limpets in your local community. It is now mid-morning on Easter Sunday and you are halfway through the Sunday papers when the Chairman of the Parish Council rings to say that he will bring the children round in 30 minutes. Do you:

a) Raid the larder for a block of Bourneville cooking chocolate which you liberally scatter round the flowerbeds, informing them that the lack of paper or brightly coloured foil is part of your drive to be more environmentally friendly.

b) Bribe your teenage children to hide your pre-ordered stock of cream eggs around the garden while your wife keeps the leg limpets busy inside.

c) Greet the Little Monsters at the front door wearing your Coneyskin slippers with the unfortunate news that the Easter Rabbit was unfortunately called away on urgent business in BunnyLand but they are welcome to come in for some really yummy Lapin Cassoulet and Lassie's Choco Drops.

May: It is your 'tweenie's Birthday. He has asked for a Pizza party. What do you do to help organize and run it?

a) Get your secretary to reserve Mama Luigi's for 20 kids and a magician to make them disappear afterwards.

b) Make the dough in the breadmaker, harvest your own tomatoes from the greenhouse, milk the cow and curdle the cheese, import the pepperoni, put up the tent and host a Make Your Own Pizza Party.

c) Book a Domino's for 20 kids and 'Kill Bill 1' and '-2' from the video shop.

June: Your wife has just given birth. Visiting hours are restricted to afternoons but England only need 250 runs to beat Australia on the last day of the Test. Do you:

a) Speak to the Ward Sister and ask for a special morning appointment to see your new baby since you are child-sitting in the afternoon.

b) Set the video and go to see your wife. It'll be replayed for the next 6 months anyway.

c) Ring every Australian you know to tell them what a good view you had and how much you understand their grief. Book a taxi to take you and the crate of Guinness to the ward so that your wife can help you celebrate.

Educating Daddy

July: It is time to get away from it all on a summer holiday. You have waited purpose-fully to book a last minute deal for the family. Do you :

a) Peruse the back pages of the News of the Screws, on your way to the interesting stuff up front, noting that Scumbucket Travel offer a cheap flat for two in the centre of Aiya Napa with a put-you-up for the kids, Happy Hour drinks at Hooters and a Brazilian Wax for you both for only £150.

b) Having put the children to bed, you search all Sunday evening until you find a gite in the Dordogne with its own pool, tennis court and a convenient 'granny annex' for your parents in law. You can catch the 11.00 am flight from your provincial airport for only £14.99 per head.

c) You find that the BudgieLand theme park on the edge of the North Yorks Moors will take the children, without parents, for a fortnight in an onsite caravan for £100 per day. You consider it a bargain and make an annual booking for the next 18 years.

August: It's time for the A-Level results to pop through the door. Your Gangly Lion is on tenterhooks because his credibility, university place and next year's allowance depend on them. What do you do?

a) Assume the worst and speak to your mate about labouring jobs in his construction company.

b) Take him to the pub for a beer, discuss the various possible outcomes and options for the future. Assure him of your support whichever way it goes.

c) Take him round the back to punch some sense into him and put his bedroom up for rent. Take the dog to the pub and bemoan current educational standards under this Government.

September: You have a long-standing date for supper at your wife's parents on the same night as the Masonic Grand Master's Dinner for which you have just received your long-awaited inaugural invitation. Do you:

a) Develop gastroenteritis on the morning of the supper, recovering just in time to get to the Masonic Hall for pre-dinner drinks.

b) Send flowers and apologies to your mother-in-law, noting that your father-in-law will approve of the strategic advancement of your career in the police service and give you a funny handshake next time you visit.

c) Dress for dinner being sure to include G String, stockings and suspenders, apron and fancy dress mask. Alternatively, if you decide to go to your in-laws instead, don't take the apron and mask.

October: The Half Term break is upon you and you have a week's holiday in hand which your wife doesn't know about. Do you:
a) Ring your golfing mates and book a week in Marbella, telling your wife that there is a super-secret corporate strategy retreat at an as yet unknown location.
b) Take the leave from work and surprise your family with a week's tennis coaching course, with on-site crèche, at La Manga.
c) Book the children into a week's arduous training camp on Dartmoor and spend a quiet week at home with your wife.

November: It is Guy Fawkes' Night at School and you have a Family ticket for the fireworks and Hog Roast thereafter. You have also won two tickets in the Works Raffle to see Menchester United v Unreal Madrid at Old Truffles. What do you do?
a) Declare that you feel that fireworks are loud and dangerous and your newfound Islamic beliefs makes it impossible for you to be present at a Hog Roast. Look up train times to Menchester.
b) Trade the tickets for a short-break weekend for two at Centre Perks and enjoy the whizzes and bangs with the best of them.
c) Declare Guy Fawkes right, but unfortunate to get caught. Arrange a similar gunpowder plot under the Menchester United dressing room.

December: It is time to arrange where and what you are going to do for Christmas as a family. Do you stay at home, go to the grandparents' or go out? Do you :
a) Go to her parents. SHE will be happy, the grandparents will be sufferable and the children will be insufferable but you'll be too inebriated to care.
b) Ask your wife where she would like to spend Christmas and go with the flow.
c) Book a table for Christmas Dinner and drinks at a local hotel. Book yourself a table and a Christmas drink in Las Vegas.

Hint: The options allow you to choose any one of the following:
a) the answer any self-respecting Dad would prefer to come up with.
b) the right answer: boring, but what Mum wants to hear
b) the 'real' answer, but you dare not admit it..
Conclusions: If you answered:
Mostly 'a's: Why did SHE marry you?
Mostly 'b's: You are a paragon or drive one.
Mostly 'c's: Your children would be better off at Barnardo's. Put Childline as option one on the house phone's speed dial.

You are meant to know by Pseudo-Osmotic Operational Process (POOP) which nights are PTA meetings, Nativity plays, swimming/tennis/violin lessons etc etc. You are expected to take appropriate action to de-conflict your diary. This also helps Mum to remain a person in her own right, and will avoid her asking your permission to leave the house, because you'll already know where she is. Of course, you will remember your annual important dates (Wedding Anniversary, HER birthday, Christmas). As the Dad, you have an unwritten duty to also think it through for the Little People and to get the presents, cards and flowers lined up for them. You will also have to surreptitiously barrage the Gangly Lions with texts to remind them that Hell hath no fury as a Mother scorned. Get yourself a family calendar – or else you're certain to end up right in the Poop.

Recognizing the Signs

When you were a bachelor, you had a finely-tuned radar that could spot an available and normally suitable girl at 50 paces. Of course the on-board radar degraded with alcohol consumption until it became confused between Coyote and Comely but in the main it served you well until you met SHE. It is an utter fallacy that men pick their wives; in truth, women let us think that we are in control while we strut around parading our physical and economic potential. Then, one of them says: "That one. I think I'll have that one" and from there on in, you're dead meat, mate. Accept the fact now, that if a woman wants a man, then she'll get him sooner or later. If you don't believe us, then ask any divorcée whose husband has left her for another woman.

Once you're married however, your radar appears to malfunction during the walk back down the aisle and all those little signs that you could spot so well across a bar (the slant of the body, the crossing of the legs, the raised eyebrow), all seem to signal utterly different meanings. Now these once easily recognisable come-ons just mean I'm just resting my back after carrying a Little Person for two hours through the grocery shopping or I'm desperate to go to the bathroom and I haven't had a chance since the baby was crying and the cat licked her bottle's teat and then the phone rang. The raised eyebrow just questions why you really had to stop for one more pint in the pub. To help you avoid any

"Oh him? He forgot to remind the children about Mother's Day...."

misunderstandings and thereby lose all the bonus points you've gained so far, here are some examples of verbal and non-verbal communication that Mum will use:

What Mummy really means - a verbal and non-verbal recognition guide

"Fine": This is the word that Mums use to end an argument when they feel they are right and you need to shut up. Never use 'fine' to describe how a

Mum looks. This will cause you to have one of those arguments that you wish never happened and forever wonder how it started in the first place.

Soft sigh: Again, not a word, but a non-verbal statement. Soft sighs mean that she is content. Your best bet is to not move or breathe, and she will stay content.

"Thanks": A Mum is thanking you. Do not faint. Just say "You're welcome."

"Five minutes": This is half an hour. It is equivalent to the five minutes that your football game or article in the newspaper is going to last before you take out the rubbish, so it's a fair trade.

"Nothing": This means 'something', often 'something important' and you should be on your toes. 'Nothing' is usually used to describe the feeling a Mum has of wanting to turn you inside out, upside down, and backwards. 'Nothing' usually signifies an argument that will last 'five Minutes' and end with 'Fine.' Remove all sharp implements from within arm's reach.

"Go ahead" (With raised eyebrows): This is a dare, not simple permission. It will result in a Mum getting upset over 'Nothing' and will end with the word 'Fine.' Tread VERY carefully.

"Go ahead" (Normal eyebrows): This means 'I give up' or 'do what you want because I don't care.' You will get a raised eyebrow 'Go Ahead' in just a few minutes, followed by 'Nothing' and 'Fine' and she will talk to you in about 'Five Minutes' when she cools off. Go to the shed and think about it.

"GO AHEAD!": At some point in the near future, you are going to be in some mighty big trouble.

Loud sigh: This is not actually a word, but is a non-verbal statement often misunderstood by Dads. A 'loud sigh' means she thinks you are an idiot at that moment, and wonders why she is wasting her time standing here and arguing with you over 'nothing.' Retreat immediately and play with the Little People.

"That's Okay": This is one of the most dangerous statements that a Mum can make to a Dad. 'That's okay' means that she wants to think long and hard before paying you back for whatever it is that you have done. 'That's okay' is often used with the word 'fine' and in conjunction with a raised eyebrow. Try flowers.

"Please do": This is not a statement, it is an offer. A Mum is giving you the chance to come up with whatever excuse or reason you have for doing whatever it is that you have done. You have a fair chance with the truth, so be careful and you shouldn't get a 'that's okay.' If you get silence, you've blown it! Shed time for a week.

"Thanks a lot": This is much different from 'Thanks.' A Mum will say: "Thanks A Lot" when she is really ticked off at you. It signifies that you have offended her in some callous way, and it will be followed by the loud sigh. Be careful not to ask what is wrong after the loud sigh, as she will only tell you "Nothing." Again, retreat immediately and deeply immerse yourself into the carefree world of a six year old. The role of Marvello, Master of the Universe, with his Fantasmagoric Ray Beam normally does the trick.

Silence: This is akin to the two minute wait for the first thermonuclear missile to hit. When a Mum responds only with silence then be very careful and VERY scared. SHE's really annoyed and you, Buster, are Ground Zero. EVACUATE! (hide in the shed until your leg limpet emissaries have negotiated a truce).

"Kneel and bow to SHE!
(and if you've got any ironing, put it over there)."

Educating Daddy

The miracle of multi-tasking

Like the Pyramids or Niagara Falls, stand in awe and do not wonder about how it happens, just accept that Mums can do it and Dads can't. Your synapses work in serial patterns whilst hers work in parallel because they have to in order to get the Mummy job done. Just be content that by the time you get your ONE thing done really well, the children will be washed, fed and tucked in, the cat will be doctored, your clothes will be laundered and ironed, and the fridge will be re-stocked with beer. Just take the rubbish out. Do NOT try to compete – it was a done deal on the Day of Creation in exchange for Pre-Menstrual Tension and the 'Pains of Childbirth' and who are you to question it? Actually, you got the better deal.

Homework

Helpful advice on improving your sex life.

During the next week :

1) Get some Soft Gushy stuff in here and your Bonus Marks will multiply all on their own. Show her that you appreciate her, and not just in lace and stockings.

2) Tell her what a good Mummy she is (Bonus Mark if you can get a Little Person to do so and Double Bonus Marks if you get it on video)

3) Simply ask her what her day was like, and listen carefully to her reply. Do not sound judgemental in any of your responses.

4) Organise a boys' trip away (no longer than two nights) and a girls' trip away for her while you look after the kids. This should be at least the same duration as the boys' trip - but the trips should NOT be simultaneous.

5) Organise a Mum's and Dad's ONLY Trip away with grandparents/good friends looking after the Little People. Bonus Mark if she is 'officially' unaware and highly delighted. Double Bonus Marks if SHE doesn't have to re-arrange all your arrangements to fit in with Scouts/swimming class/piano lessons/ballet/Pony Club/Kennels. Don't worry about the lace and stockings, SHE'll know, SHE's human too!

15
D is for Difficult
No-one said it was going to be easy

Caveat: This chapter is necessarily different in tone to the other chapters. The subject matter encompasses issues that cannot be avoided, even though most Dads would rather that Mum dealt with them. It is necessarily political at times because difficult issues are often the result of nonsensical policies or the absence of any sensible approach. We would also be accused of dodging the issues if we didn't address some of the most difficult questions that your Little People are going to pose. They'll do this, not just to make your life awkward nor to try to embarrass you, but because they are going to either experience these issues directly or observe them at close quarters. Whichever it is, they will want some form of explanation and you are going to have to provide it. You are the Daddy, after all, and you're meant to know the answers. So we'd better have a look at some of them now so that you'll have a fighting chance when the bombshells start landing around you. Remember, this is NOT meant to be a compendium of 'everything you'll need to know', but rather provides a pointer in the right direction for each topic.

Death

Surprisingly little is known about variation in injury rates and types by age and gender, and how this differs for fatal and non-fatal injuries of juveniles. Given that our children are our greatest treasures, surely we should have wondered by now what the greatest threats to them are and what we have to do to protect them? Logically, if we know what the problem is then we can do something about it. If we simply guess at what the problem is, then we stand the risk of missing something and allowing the loss of (or serious injury to) youngsters that might otherwise have been avoided. Is this negligence on our part to date? Would it help reduce the NHS bill? Would it help more parents to love and cherish their greatest treasures?

The Greatest Threats

The greatest global risks to the health of the young are pneumonia, gastroenteritis and malaria. In England however, the major threats are no longer disease based. Injury and poisoning are the major causes of death and disability in children and young people (0-19 years old). According to a Draft Paper by the Department of Social Medicine, University of Bristol injury and poisoning in England account for around 30% of all deaths in this age group and, between 1991 and 2000, resulted in 11,693 deaths and 1,519,291 hospital admissions in 0–19 year-olds. While motor vehicle traffic accidents (MVTAs) were the most common cause of injury deaths overall, falls were responsible for the greatest number of hospital admissions. Changing patterns of risk were seen by age and for boys and girls. Motor vehicle occupant deaths increased with age but hospital admissions for falls, suffocation and drowning decreased. Suicide and deliberate self-harm (DSH) featured prominently in the older age groups, with suicide deaths three times as common among boys but hospital admission for DSH more than twice as common among girls. Admissions and deaths caused by motor vehicles and pedal cycles were much more common among boys. The key findings from this important piece of research are that:

- Injury among England's children and young people is a serious concern. Each year in this age group more than twice as many die from injuries as from cancer.
- On average, injury in 0–19 year-olds in England causes one death every 8 hours and one hospital admission every three minutes.
- Motor Vehicle Traffic Accidents account for 40% of injury deaths of children and teenagers but only 6% of injury-related hospital admissions.
- Falls account for 3% of injury deaths but 33% of injury-related hospital admissions.
- Boys are at higher risk than girls of death and hospital admission for virtually all causes of injury across all age groups.
- 45% of total injury deaths are among boys aged 15-19 years old.
- 57% of all transport-related injury admissions in 5–14 year old boys and 52% of those in 5-9 year old girls involved pedal cycles. Bicycles are involved in 35% of all unintentional injury deaths of school-aged children.
- 18% of all transport accidents in 10-19 year old girls involved riding animals or animal-drawn vehicles; they were 10 times as likely as boys of this age to

be involved in these accidents.
• 40% of girls' hospital admissions for injury at 15-19 years are for deliberate self-harm.
• Assault accounts for only 4% of injury deaths and 5% of hospital admissions. However, it is the cause of 15% of injury admissions among 15–19 year-old boys.

So what? Having established the major effects and their possible causes, it behoves us to ask what we should therefore be doing to mitigate them and so help to protect our youngsters further if possible:

1) Boys will be boys: They will climb trees – but are more likely to injure themselves than to kill themselves. Girls love riding horses and ponies and there are inherent dangers, though these are also more likely to lead to injury than death. There is little we can do other than take the natural precautions that parents have traditionally taken – but we can be there when they try to climb the tree or jump the jump. Too many modern children get *gravel rash* where parents are easily inclined to drop them off and accelerate away to do something for themselves, expecting somebody else to take care of, and responsibility for, their children.

2) MVTA – the big killer: It doesn't really matter whether your children are the innocent pedestrians or the onboard passenger victims of poor driving. Dead is dead no matter which way it happens. It has been found that young people are greater risk-takers because their brains do not fully develop until they are about 25 years old. Of particular note is the relationship between development of the dorsal-lateral prefrontal cortex, the bit behind the brow, and driving ability. Whilst this might be an evolutionary factor in preparing young people to leave their families and fend for themselves, it also means that they are less likely to consider all the factors when they are driving or riding in a car or on a bike. Teach them from the earliest stage to wear a safety belt. Despite the fact that it has been the law for over 20 years now, it is not difficult to see children bouncing freely around inside many vehicles on a daily basis. Given the fact that MVTAs account for more than 40% of injury deaths of children, perhaps we should be lobbying harder for the incorporation of specific (no cost) restrictions for new or young drivers. These could perhaps include clear speed restrictions (under 50mph?), mandatory Green 'P' plates (P for Provisional Driver meaning 'Watch out for me I'm not a learner, but I am new at this, give me a lot of space'), limiting engine size/power of cars driven by new drivers and enforcing an absolute No drink rule as opposed to the current (possible two drink) limit. Any infringement would automatically incur a one year ban and a retest would then be required. It is a recognized fact that children under the age of nine (especially boys) have difficulty in judging the speed and distance of cars, have poor peripheral vision and therefore have a greater vulnerability to being knocked over by vehicles. So, one of the best ways of keeping your Little People safe is to make sure that they know how dangerous it can be to play on or around roads and that you know how fast you are going in areas where you are likely to be near children on the roadside. In much of the USA, where there is plenty of open space, children are actually banned from playing in the street. In the UK, where we have much less open space, we should perhaps rely on greater education and sensible driving for the sake of greater freedom. Finally, and possibly most importantly, make sure that you teach them about not drinking and driving and remind them about Safety Rule Number One and the other Cardinal Rules.

3) Bicycle Safety: What we used to call 'cycling proficiency' has gone out of fashion in recent years. Perhaps it should be re-introduced, and youngsters should be given an incentive to gain a recognized road safety qualification? Roads in the UK are now too busy, and thus potentially too lethal, not to have some form of safety license. If the dangerous and poor road safety standards shown by most cyclists in busy city centres are anything to go by then such licenses are definitely needed. More cycle paths could easily be included as part of the statutory planning requirements for local councils, especially in areas of new or re-development. These would bring great benefits for the local and global environment as well. The Dutch have shown us the way here, albeit on a billiard-board of a country, so why not follow their lead?

4) Deliberate Self-Harm in older girls: This surprisingly modern phenomenon appears to emanate from a perceived lack of self–respect and self-esteem among girls. So why should this occur over the past 20 years? Is this the influence of the media, the desire for pseudo-iconic wannabe status and the perception of failure if a girl's face/figure/fashion sense doesn't match the dream that is thrust down their throats 24 hours per day, seven days a week and 365 days a year on TV, radio, the internet, in magazines and even bus stop advertising? A Hollywood celebrity ideal has been reinforced by the perception that you can "have it all" without effort or talent. This perception may have been driven, in part, by the influence of the Lottery and by reality television. These offer images of instant stardom and lifestyle, which are being vicariously lived by ordinary people through TV and via a growing pile of 'Through the Keyhole' glossies like 'Hello!' and 'OK!' magazines. Is there a total disconnect between aspiration and what is realistically attainable for the ordinary teenage girl in UK society? It is not possible (or even desirable) that all of us should be rich, famous, beautiful and thin.

A recent survey of the 'Emotional Health' of 2,000 14 and 15 year old girls by University College London, commissioned by Bliss Magazine found that they feel under pressure and unable to cope. Nine out of ten said that they feel depressed (42% of them regularly), over 33% said that they were unhappy or miserable and a disturbing 6% felt that 'life was not worth living'. The main reasons given for such attitudes were:

1) Too much pressure to look good (94%)
2) Too much homework (84%)
3) Too much pressure to succeed academically (62%)
4) A rise in broken families/divorce (52%)
5) Drugs and alcohol too readily available (42%)

Interestingly, 37% came from broken homes or single parent families and only 32% felt "greatly loved by their parents". So, are we right to lust after a modern lifestyle for our whole society? Or would it be wiser to advise and guide our teenage daughters to stop trying so hard to be something they are not and to be content with who and what they are and can become? There is a high price to pay for this wannabe society, even beyond the alarming rise in teenage 'self-harming.' One out of every eight US citizens (36 million out of 288 million) currently live below the poverty line (equivalent to £10,460 pa for a family of four), and general prosperity in the UK masks a growing gap between rich and poor, and a growing gap between 'dream and reality'.

5) Assault in older boys: despite the low level of injury deaths and hospital admissions as a percentage of the total, the relatively high percentage (15%) of injury admissions specifically due to assault alone among 15–19 year-old boys is significant. Of course this is when they are in the prime of their Young Lion stage and are most likely to be testing themselves against one another, but how much of this physical bravado is fuelled by drink or drugs? Is there not a more controlled outlet that might be found? Hard physical exercise in a competitive arena drains excess energy and aggression and can inculcate positive competitive qualities such as team loyalty, discipline, and co-operative working. This kind of 'positive tribalism' will only be possible with the input of qualified community coaches and with clubs and playing fields to play on. While the major political parties have all made encouraging noises about supporting and expanding sporting opportunities for young people, this rhetoric has been accompanied by the selling of school and community sports facilities and the reduction of sports funding. So much for social engineering.

Traumatic Behavioural Response Chart

If you are lucky, the first encounter your Little People will have with the Grim Reaper will be from afar via the newspaper, television or radio. They will not understand it, but will accept it as a given fact, if you introduce them to it as a natural part of the cycle of life. Remind them about Bambi's mother or Simba's father in the Lion King, show them things in the garden that grow, bloom, wither and die and let them know that everything has to follow the same path at one time of another. This includes you, their mum and, in due course, even themselves. But make sure that they know that there is nothing to fear about death and that it shouldn't happen for some time. The difficult bit of course, comes when early or unexpected death impacts directly on their lives – coming too close to their inner sanctum of security.

If this happens you will have to simultaneously deal with shock, fear, anger, recrimination and total disorientation. This emotional cycle is not particular to the reaction to death, but will occur to some degree in reaction to divorce, dismissal, arrest or any other shocking event which arrives unexpectedly.

The normal phases of behaviour are:

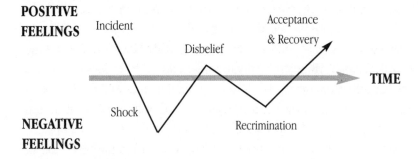

These are completely normal emotions and everyone experiences them as part of the human brain's way of rationalising abnormal or traumatic experiences that do not fit the accepted picture of normal daily life. For children, this can be tremendously hard, especially if the person who has died has been one of the immediate family and, worst of all, if it was Mummy. Your best tools are love, patience, understanding, soft-spoken words and lots and lots of hugs. If you are grieving too then share your grief with them but be careful not to share the recrimination and anger that will inevitably follow. Let them know that it is OK to cry, regardless of age or gender, and that thinking and talking about it is perfectly alright – especially for someone or something you love and miss. Your duty as their Dad is to absorb their loss and help them through the most difficult of times. Religious conviction can be a great bulwark against such a loss and there are many brilliant pieces of literature that can help in such difficult times. These range from unrestrained expressions of grief such as W.H. Auden's "Stop all the clocks..." (IX of Twelve Songs, and perhaps best known now from the funeral in the film 'Four Weddings and a Funeral') to pure celebrations and thanksgivings for life as in Schiller's "Ode to Joy". The greatest kindness though is to help heal the wound created by the loss of a loved one. Your aim should be to transform negative emotions into positive ones, which is perhaps best done through stirring memories of good times, good fun and laughter together. Hopefully, if you have followed the fundamental lesson of Chapter 1, you will still have three handholds and a strong Friendship Lifeline to keep you and your Little People on the Rock-face of Life.

Divorce

Divorce can induce trauma similar to that induced by death – but accentuated by circumstances and by the fact that your partner is still alive and often kicking. The biggest problem is responding to the bewilderment and fears of the Little People while simultaneously managing the feelings of rejection between you and your partner. The "Are you divorcing us as well Dad?" question is merely symptomatic of their fear of rejection and of the loss of the security and comfort that having both you and their Mum around to provide, protect, care for and guide them represented. Actually, most of the problems you will encounter will also be experienced by those Dads who live a form of self-enforced temporary divorce through weekday absence as city commuters or shift-workers. So don't think that you are alone in trying to cope with them just because you and their Mum have decided to split up.

Some 44% of those surveyed in the Teen Emotional Health Survey 2005, whose parents had separated or divorced, said that their parents' separation had 'knocked them emotionally' and a further 11% said that they had found it 'devastating'. Worryingly, 40% said that they did not have a happy family.

Acrimonious divorce may well exacerbate everybody's feelings of rejection and should be avoided if at all possible, not only for the sake of the children but also for the sake of the bank balance. It is not divorce *per se* that damages relationships but the manner and environment in which it is conducted. Most importantly, remember that the Little People may be the smallest pieces on the chess board, but they are NOT pawns for you and the Black Queen to manoeuvre around. You may well be at your wits end with their Mum, but ask yourself 'Am I really angry at the children too?' If not, leave them out of the arguments. If you are, then seek a child psychologist – for yourself.

*"And you can tell Batwoman that I want regular access
to Robin and custody of the Batmobile."*

Maintenance will be a major part of the ongoing rows, and on this issue, we would only refer you back to Chapter 2 ('It takes Two to Tango'). All your responsibilities won't go away just because you or SHE did; you still have to provide for the children as part of the unwritten contract you inadvertently agreed to when you made them. You have to pay your fair share when it's due, and we are not going to discuss what's fair here, you can pay a lawyer exorbitant fees to do that for you. The greatest things that you can give your Little People to help them through the trauma of divorce are free anyway: extra time, extra love, extra understanding and lots of patient explanation. If you can understand their pain, anger and loss then one day they might understand what happened and how you both tried to do the best for them. Bear in mind though that only 7% of divorced Dads in the UK are granted custody of the children and four out of ten lose touch with them completely after a divorce. Incredibly, one in four children live in single parent homes, imposing a £15 Billion annual cost on the UK taxpayer, who funds the resulting single parent benefit payments. It would therefore be in everybody's interest to make divorce as difficult as possible – or at least a darn sight more difficult than it appears to be at present. This might reduce current single parent benefit payments and might also reduce the overall divorce rate. Similarly, dual parent upbringing, where both parents take an active role, seems to produce healthier, better socialised children who undoubtedly make better future citizens.

A fair deal?

The current legislative system appears to be biased against men when it comes to awarding custody of the children in a divorce settlement. Whilst UK society appears to be changing slowly, there remains an automatic assumption that Mum is the most suitable primary carer for the children, and that she should have the greater say in doctrinal issues. More damaging to the Dad/Child relationship is that Mum's still gain a disproportionate share of access to the children. It is not surprising that most divorced fathers feel a deep sense of injustice. This is reflected by the growth of organisations such as Fathers4Justice, and is echoed in a range of parenting websites. Many divorced Dads have a sense of being 'ripped off' by a society that demands that he hands over 50% of his possessions, pays an additional % of his income in maintenance and then has less than 50% of timed access to the children. There appears to be little, if any, recognition of the emotional penalty paid by Dads for the lost opportunities for contact with their Little People at bathtime, bedtime, and other (daily) precious moments. It is acknowledged that children who have more post-separation contact with fathers adjust better, and are healthier and more stable. We should be trying to maximise contact with both parents rather than bias access in favour of one parent. Few children understand the implications of divorce, so it is up to us to get it right so that they do not suffer. Boys especially need role models, based on men who they know, trust and love. It is in the interests of the child that he/she should feel equally loved and valued by both parents. This is impossible if one parent has only limited time and access in which to reinforce that message.

Exercise 19

Divorce Value Proposition

1) List those people you know who have been through a 'friendly' divorce. List the benefits that the divorce has brought them. Calculate the real winners. Hint, delete: Yourself, your partner, the children, the grandparents, your friends, and your workmates. Insert: one bedroomed apartment landlords, solicitors, MacDadsville, Sunday Matinee Cinema ticket sales.

2) Ask yourself: " Was it worth it or could they have found a way round it?" Go back and read the statistics and responses from the Teen Emotional Health survey 2005.

3) Lobby your MP to make marriage illegal, or at least a darned sight more difficult, thereby removing much of the suffering caused by divorce and the ease with which it appears to be used to rectify hasty decisions. Campaign for a media contribution to all divorce settlements for unrealistically insisting that all marriages are made in Hollywood.

Disease and Disability

Like Death, there are some things in Life that just happen for no apparent reason and about which we can do very little. Children will suffer from coughs, colds, chicken pox and measles. These complaints are uncomfortable at the time but, in most cases, they will be quickly forgotten. Use these minor ailments to help explain other more serious diseases when they observe or experience them for themselves. You might also say how lucky they are that they do not suffer such things on a permanent basis, and ask them how they would feel if they did catch such a disease or had an accident and lost their ability to walk, hear or see. If you want a ready, and humbling, example of how people disabled by a wide range of ailments can still show tremendous bravery and fortitude, then look no further than the Paralympics. Make a point of comparing the times, distances and records with those of other Olympians.

Disability is more of a description of minds and opinions than of physical attributes – your job is to ensure that your children are not so afflicted. Remember that your Little People are always watching, listening and repeating your actions, so the best example you can give them is through your daily life.

Set them an example by how you deal with those who try to live their lives while carrying such an extra load.

Discrimination

Everybody discriminates in one way or another. You will naturally hope that your children will have better housing, food, education, clothing, medical care and opportunities but how you attempt to progress things for your own Tribe over the interests of non-Tribal members is important. Your Little People will learn from you and those that they look up to as guides and mentors and, as with disease and disability, if you practise senseless discrimination based upon colour, age, creed, religion or sexuality then so too will they. There is enough brutality going on in current inter-Tribal wars across 50% of the globe. Don't add to it – do something positive and join the Sapiens in the other 50%. Who knows, perhaps they'll extend the discrimination range to include Old Men in future? So do yourself and all the other Dads a favour and teach your children to extend their respect and toleration to Wrinklies well before you get there.

Dishonour

"Treasure your reputation and teach them to treasure theirs."

There are 4 major ways in which your offspring could "lose their name" and their reputation by earning the sobriquet of Liar, Thief, Cheat or Bully.

Liar and Thief!

Learning about honesty, be it in word or deed, should be one of the earliest and most fundamental lessons in a Little Person's life and it's up to you and Mum to teach them, with additional input from your wider circle of family, friends and teachers. But, the basic responsibility is yours. You will find it easy if you start right from the earliest age, when they don't want to give back the prettiest doll or newest 'Starbuster' toy on leaving the Day Care Centre or don't want to admit to having done something that they know they shouldn't have done. This will progress through to petty pilfering of sweets in shops and down the slippery slope to bigger and glossier items and more intricate stories and lies as their inbuilt honesty mechanism naturally withers and dies, mainly through your lack of interest and concern. Little people need regulation and it's primarily your responsibility to give it to them, not the responsibility of their Teachers, not that of the Police and certainly not of the State. It's one of your fundamental responsibilities so accept it and take sufficient interest in your Little People to apply it to them. (Hint: Discuss it fully with Mum first, she'll tell you what you need to know and, if you're reading this from the comfort of your own cell, ask her at the next visiting day). Remember to tell her and them that just because you did something wrong it doesn't mean that you love them any the less.

Cheat!

Don't cheat at sport and, more importantly, don't allow or encourage them to cheat either. Children do as children see. If you teach them to cheat in their games and on the sports field then you are also actively teaching them to cheat in the other aspects of their life. Equally when you discuss the behaviour of their role models, heroes and mentors, be sure to show your approval or disapproval of how they behave. Some of our public bodies (eg FIFA,)do nobody any favours when they refuse to castigate national heroes and role models for their drug use or deliberate foul play, even allowing them to retain the Captaincy of an England national team at a major sport. Cheating at sport will never be forgotten and will often be mentioned in the locker room, especially when you aren't there, so make sure that your little players are not subject to such comment.

Failure

Dealing with failure is all part of growing up. They have to learn to accept the moment of defeat as easily as they enjoy the moment of victory, and it is up to you to show them the way. There's a vital lesson in looking another man or woman in the eye and saying 'Well done!' meaning it and knowing that their victory was fairly won. No matter how hard the tears of disappointment cascade from your treasured Little Person, the short-term loss will be rewarded twenty-fold later in life – especially when it is their turn to be the victor. It is often said in business that you can tell a man by how he plays his golf. Why else do you think so many people spend so much time learning how to play that particular game? It's really a cunning recruitment and personnel development tool developed by a canny Jock who wanted to suss out his business rivals, have four hours uninterrupted time with a prospective customer and who didn't want to pay headhunter's fees.

Bully!

The last major way in which your Little People could earn a social stigma as children is to incur the dubious title of 'bully'. Modern day definitions of bullying have become more enlightened since the days of Flashman and now recognize moral and mental torture as well as the traditional bashing or hair-pulling in the playground. But children still need to be taught what the proper limits are so that they can recognize when they are getting near to what is, or is not, acceptable and so that they know when to draw back. Equally, from a victim's point of view, they need to know when and how to cry for help, without earning the equally damning stigma of 'cry-baby', 'tell-tale' or 'wimp' from their peers.

If punishment is meted out, then a suitable programme of rehabilitation for the future is equally vital. This ensures an understanding of the greater effects of the bullying, but also actively includes the victim in all future activities making sure that they are regarded as worthy individuals in their own right. There is lots of good advice now available through schools and on the Internet, for example at the national charity www.ParentlinePlus.org.uk, which can help both you and your child when bullying occurs. Remember that it can, and does, happen to girls as well as to boys. It might well be that the higher incidence of suicide and deliberate self-harm in older girls is the result of lower self-esteem brought on by bullying, in one form or another, that was not recognized or dealt with at an earlier stage. Finally, it is worth reminding your Little Ones that the honour codes are never forgotten and that the stigmas of liar, thief, cheat and bully will stay with them for life if you allow it.

> *"There are no medals on Earth for getting the Difficult Questions right, but heaps of gongs for getting them wrong."*

Homework

1) Discuss each of these topics with Mum so that you have a game plan for when the Difficult Questions come at you. Hopefully, you will stop short of needing to discuss the details of divorce from Mum, but you should have worked out a ready response for when your Little People observe other family structures disintegrating. If you have had to address one or more of these areas, then question how well you dealt with it and how you would tackle the other issues in future.

2) Think of all those people who you knew at school who you now remember as either a liar, thief, cheat or bully. Promise yourself that your children will NOT be remembered as such in 20 years time. Decide what you have to do in order to keep that promise for them.

Educating Daddy

16
Putting Your Feet Up

Well, Graduation is just over the page and it's almost time to wrap the Dad's Course that you have, hopefully, been following through this book. You'll need some easy methods to judge your performance once you've left Daddy's College so we'll start with what you're trying to achieve, stating your objectives in good old business-speak. Consider this book as a Management Training Handbook for 'Your Family Incorporated.' You are the CEO: setting the agenda and the standards, providing the leadership and the wherewithal, propagating and protecting the brand (the family name) and training your team. Mum is of course the Operations Director, Finance Director, Marketing Director and Manufacturing Director (but that's another story). Fatherhood is thus about leadership and management of the family brand, finances, product and team members - and survival at shareholder meetings.

You and Mum will have Board Meetings, probably once the other team members have been put to bed. Here you will decide on company strategy and operational policy, current finances/cash flow and future resourcing. This is also your opportunity to discuss how best to manufacture your product and market the brand. A host of personnel related issues such as remuneration rates, sickness and holidays will come up as well. Expect to have to regularly brief the Non-Executive Directors (grandparents), and any other shareholders who hold vested interests in the family brand – noting of course that your offspring become fully independent shareholders in due course with full voting rights and an oft-used voice to question company policy at shareholder meetings. Suffice to say that what you need is:

The Dad's Vision Statement

"A Dad should deliver a considerate, fair, free-thinking, healthy, honest, individual, just, kind, likeable, stable, well-informed, and well-mannered Little Person into the Real World, who can stand up for themselves and who will be a good Dad or Mum to their own Little People in due course."

In order to do this, you will need

The Dad's Mission Statement

> *"To educate, protect, provide and socialise your Little People whilst maintaining a good relationship with their Mother so that you can have a long and peaceful life together."*

...If you can do that, you'll have done a good job. Well done Dad. You can now put your feet up, for a couple of minutes at least, hum the School Hymn (See beginning of book) and progress to:

Graduation

You should now refer to the Chief Examiner, otherwise known as Mum, to see whether you are ready to graduate. She will be fully aware that you are taking this course. SHE probably bought you the Student Handbook in the first place or booked your place on the Course, and will have noticed your changes in behaviour and conversation as you have progressed through the Chapters. If this is NOT the case, then refer back to Chapter 1 and read the words this time, don't just colour in the cartoons. Note that, no matter how well you have done on the coursework during the Chapters, there is one Key Question for the Chief Examiner to answer that defines whether or not you are ready to graduate:

Would you confidently leave him alone with your Little People for a week?

If the answer is a definite yes, then well done. You have obviously either read the whole Handbook and put the principles into practice as you progressed, or you were spectacularly well adapted to the role anyway. Congratulate your wife and your mother. If however, you received a qualified yes or even a no, and some Dads do, then take the opportunity to ask why and work on those areas. Remember that there may come a day when you have to take control of the Little People for a week or longer, so take this opportunity to sort out not only what you can do, but also to work out what specialist help you might need. Invest in a suitable insurance policy now for that Babysitter, Cook, Cleaner, Day Care Assistant, Ironing lady, Maid, Nanny, Nurse and Valet that you currently call 'the Wife'.

Homework

During the next week. take your wife out and celebrate your success as parents, and plan where you're going to go on that cruise together – without the children.

Afternote

The final Blinding Glimpse of the Obvious
"You will never complete the task. Being a Dad is a job for life."

Even after they have left home you will find that they will ring to confirm everything that you've tried to pump into them in the previous years, or you'll call them to make sure that they are applying it correctly. And then, you just start helping them with the grandchildren – but at least you can then hand them back to their parents at the end of the day...

A Final Word for the Chief Examiner (AKA Mummy in residence)

Your personal student will largely be the product of a bespoke development programme where you are both designer and tailor. When you got him on approval his latent fatherhood tendencies were probably pretty well hidden and mainly the result of his Mum's conscious input and his Dad's unconscious influence. Few men are taught to be Dads; few Grandads call them up and stop over for the first few weeks after childbirth or offer a continuous programme of hints and paternal advice. By and large, men just muddle through doing the best they can and learning en route about what works and what doesn't, which is why Number One Child is always the test case, Number Two Child can hide in the middle and Number Three has to prove his worth but generally gets an easier time from more relaxed parents. Irish Catholic parents can apply for extra Chapters for Numbers Four, Five, Six and Seven. BUT, no matter how well house-trained he was when you got him, or how well you may think you have upgraded him since throwing out his pile of soft porn mags, black book and photos of his old girlfriends, he will never be perfect.

He was not born to be a Mum and never will be; he was born to be a Dad so let him do the things that Dads are meant to do and help him to do them well. Do not expect him to be a replacement Mum, he never will be, doesn't want to be and will make an utterly appalling job of it. If you do feel confident enough to leave him alone with the children for a week, you can expect him to have fed them, clothed them, cleaned them, got them to school/Cubs/ballet/football /swimming, read them stories, helped with their homework and put them to bed at a reasonable time. Just do not expect him to have cleaned the house as well. So, when you return, refreshed from your much-needed time away, to see him and them surfing happily upon a sea of domestic chaos, kiss him softly and say "Well done, darling!" because he's just done what he thought good Dads should do.

Daddy's College Homework Checksheet

To be marked by Mum (1 point per box, plus bonuses)　　　SCORE

Chapter 1 - Fundamentals

Does he do something physically active each day?

Did he spend at least one hour in your company? (with no distractions)

Did he spend at least 30 minutes playing with each of the children?

Did he get home to see the children for at least an hour BEFORE bedtime?

Did he read them a story of their choice (Bonus Mark)?

Did he create a Change Jar and has he started using it?

Has he opened a Savings Account for each child?

Chapters 2 & 3 - Birth and after

Did he talk to another new Dad about what's about to hit him?

If it was in the pub, did he take you with him? (Bonus Mark)

Has he cancelled all Boys Trips Away for the next 3 months? (Bonus Mark)

Has he come out of Self-Denial yet? (Bonus Mark if he's stopped crying)

Chapter 4 - Sharing the load

Did he send you off to do something/see a friend?

Did HE look after the children for a whole day/weekend/week?

Are they still alive and unmaimed? (Bonus Mark)

Chapter 5 - Playing with them

Did he play ducks and boats in the bath or build a 'den' with the children?

Was the dog/cat/hamster included? Was the Vet or Doctor called?

Did he spend at least One Hour playing with each of the children?

Did he take out a Board Game and play it with all of the children?

How many pieces got eaten? (subtract a mark for each one)

Did he spend time with each child following one of their activities?

Did he sit down and have 'Tea' with the Little People?

Did you all have Sunday Lunch as a 'real' meal? ☐

Are his manners OK? ☐

Does everybody in the newspaper appear to have sprouted

moustaches, beards and spectacles? ☐

Has one of your Little People suddenly got a moustache, beard & spectacles? ☐

Has he been through the SMART access rules with each of the Children? ☐

Has he taken the children to the Local Library? ☐

Did he get himself a book? ☐

Has he got enough crayons for it? ☐

Chapter 6 – Money Matters

Has he made a Will? ☐

Have You? Is it up to date with the state of your marriage? ☐

Have you nominated Guardians for the children? ☐

Has he explained and introduced Dad 's Tax? ☐

Have you (collectively) chosen a family charity for this year? ☐

Has he done anything for charity this year? ☐

Has he included the children in a Charitable activity? ☐

Chapter 7 – Explaining Things

Has he built something with your child. (Model car/Dolls House)? ☐

Did he take the children to an Activity Museum or a Farmyard? ☐

Did he make realistic farmyard noises? Was he asked to leave the Museum? ☐

Does he know where the Local Library is located? ☐

Did he get the children registered for a Library Card? ☐

Did he get one for himself? (Bonus Mark) ☐

Did he get one for you? (Double Bonus marks) ☐

Has he invented a new Tall Tale of his own? ☐

Did your Little Person laugh out loud.? ☐

Did you? (Bonus mark if you half -believed it as well) ☐

Has he been crawling round the house trying to get into trouble? ☐

Has he got a separate (Lockable) store cupboard for toxic items? ☐

Educating Daddy

Has he bought a Home/Child-oriented First Aid Book? ☐
Doe he know basic First Aid? Do you? ☐
Has he ever taken the children to work for the day? ☐
Have you 'vetted' his Secretary or the girls in Accounts? ☐

Chapter 8 – Making Friends with them
Did he take the children to school? ☐
Does he know the name of their Class Teacher? ☐
Does he know how they are getting on in class? (Bonus Mark) ☐
Did he sit down and go through their last Report with them? ☐
Has he watched them play in a match? ☐
Has he read them their favourite book or listened to their favourite record? ☐
Did he take them somewhere new, that you haven't been to either? ☐
Does he know his alphabet? Did he play the alphabet game with them? ☐
Did he get to Z without losing their interest or using a reference book? ☐

Chapter 10, 11, 12 – Sex, and Drugs, and Rock n' Roll, and the rest
Has he discussed Sex Education for the children with you? ☐
Has he discussed it with them? ☐
Has he answered their questions? ☐
Have you explained to him what the real answers should be? ☐
Have you both discussed who takes drugs that they know? ☐
Do you need to take further action? ☐
Has he listened to a record of their choice with them? ☐
Did he get them to listen to a classical record with him? (Bonus mark) ☐
Did he go through the current Top Ten Chart with them? ☐
Has he discussed sensible drinking limits with them? ☐
Was he sober at the time? ☐
Does he know about sensible drinking limits? ☐
Has he explained about guns to them, whether or not you own any? ☐
Has he organized a Family Film Night -with an educational selection of films? ☐
Have you and the children stopped having nightmares? ☐

Chapter 13 - Handling them when things went wrong

Did he go down the Gym with a scribbled list and come back with a smile? ☐

Has he been a lot nicer since then? ☐

Have some strange people with pickaxe handles been hanging around lately? ☐

Have you discussed smacking with him? ☐

Do you have an agreed domestic disciplinary policy? Have you discussed it? ☐

Have you tried bondage? ☐

Did he show you a "Count the Cost" card? Was he suitably ashamed? ☐

Did you reap a sufficient reward? ☐

Chapter 14 - Handling you

Has he been inordinately loving since he read this chapter? ☐

Has he demonstrated his appreciation of you as a Mum? ☐

Have any of your Little People recently told you what a good Mum you are? ☐

Did he get it on video? ☐

Has he organised a Boys trip away? ☐

Has he organised a Girls Trip away for you while he looks after the children? ☐

When are you two going away together without them? ☐

Have you had to make any of the arrangements? (Double marks if not) ☐

Have you packed the lace, stockings and baby oil? ☐

Chapter 15 - D is for Difficult

Did he discuss Death, Disease/Disability, Discrimination and Dishonour? ☐

Have you discussed Divorce? ☐

Should you? ☐

If he's had to deal with one of these problems already, did he do it well? ☐

Chapter 16 - Putting his feet up

Has he taken you out to dinner to celebrate your success so far? ☐

Would you like him to attend another workshop or presentation? ☐

NOW GO TO THE FINAL SCORECARD ...

FINAL SCORECARD

Tot up the marks scored in the homework checksheets presented on pages 194-197, including any bonus points.

Interpreting the result:

100: Cheat! 97 is the maximum score with bonuses.
87+: Excellent. I'll keep hold of this one for the time being.
67+: Very Good. I'll just tweak the following areas.
57+: Good. Shows potential. Now, if we can get these things right.
45-56: Average. Could improve on...
25-44: Poor. MUST improve on...
Less than 24: Untrainable. Send Me Another.
            (Send SAE to Daddy's College)

Assuming a bare pass mark of 25 or more, answer the following:

Key Question for the Chief Examiner:

  "Would you confidently leave him alone with your Little People for a whole week?"

Yes? He may graduate. Sign and issue the certificate opposite

No? Return for another Course of Instruction concentrating on:

....

I certify that ....has passed his initial training as a Daddy and may now be safely trusted with his own Little People in various stages of growth for limited periods of time without the close supervision of either his or their Mum.

Signed.. Dated...............................
Chief Examiner (aka Mummy in Residence)
Examiner's Authorisation Code......(Found on Marriage Certificate)

DADDY'S COLLEGE

It is hereby certified that it appears by the Register of the Ancient Congregation of Doctors and Regent Masters of the College of Daddies that

after having satisfied all the conditions prescribed in that respect by the Statutes of the College, and having followed an approved programme in Paternal Studies
was admitted to the degree of

Ex **BACHELOR OF DADDYHOOD**

As witness our hands this .... day of .... 200.

Peter Pater

(Mummy)
Chief Examiner

(Peter Pater, PhD)
Principal, Daddy's College

Educating Daddy

Summary of Blinding Glimpses of the Obvious

Scattered through the book are some 45 pieces of obvious but vitally important common sense advice. These are the 'Blinding Glimpses of the Obvious' mentioned in the introduction. In the text they are always presented in bold, italicised type. They are summarised here, with the page numbers on which they appear, in order to serve as a bite-sized revision guide.

BGO 1) No one ever dies saying "I wish I'd spent more time in the Office". P.8

BGO 2) You are not perfect, nor are you ever likely to be. P.9

BGO 3) The ONLY thing stopping you from being a good Dad is YOU (and your perception of what is important). P.9

BGO 4) All things are replaceable, unless they cannot be bought. P.14

BGO 5) SHE can give birth on her own, but SHE shouldn't have to..... P.22

BGO 6) Your baby will decide when it is coming – but it won't book an appointment. P.23

BGO 7) SHE cannot control her depression. P.29

BGO 8) Babies don't cry for no reason, you just need to find the reason, and then do something about it. P.32

BGO 9) Becoming a Dad is not hard, but being a Dad can be. P.37

BGO 10) You are the most important influence in your children's lives. P.43

BGO 11) If you don't care about their manners, then they won't either. P.44

BGO 12) Skin is washable. P.46

BGO 13) Little People are really very resilient and tend to bounce back. P.47

BGO 14) Play with them when they ask you

- because one day they won't ask you anymore, you'll be asking them. P.51

BGO 15) You are the best toy your child has ever been given. P.52

BGO 16) If it's electronic you need to turn it on, if it's on paper you need to open it, but you will still need to be able to read it. P.63

BGO 17) The most important thing you can give your children is your time. P.67

BGO 18) Your children are your most precious possession. So treasure them. P.75

BGO 19) Hugs and cuddles cost nothing, so give them freely. P.78

BGO 20) If you don't sort out your Will, then a Lawyer Will. P.84

BGO 21) Your children will never learn about charity if they never see you practising it. P.85

BGO 22) Little People love to know how things work. P.87

BGO 23) Education can never be taken from you and you should never give it up. P.89

BGO 24) To you, work is a necessity. To them, it is a distraction. P.95

BGO 25) Your children are with you for life, you will never be rid of them. P.98

BGO 26) Little People get VERY tired between 4 and 6 o' clock in the evening. P.100

BGO 27) You are the Head of the House, but you don't have to prove it as soon as you come home from work. P.100

BGO 28) You are the best filter for Internet access and content. P.104

BGO 29) Find a good mentor for your teenagers, before they find a bad one. P.115

BGO 30) Your daughter IS going to have sex. It's just a matter of where, when and with whom. P.122

BGO 31) The only hands you lay on a girl (or a child) are KIND hands. P.123

BGO 32) The only place to get drugs is from a doctor. P.127

BGO 33) If they don't rebel somehow, then how will they test themselves? P.130

BGO 34) Pickling your liver does NOT make it last longer. P.131

BGO 35) Plan to win the War, not a single battle. P.134

BGO 36) Don't make a threat unless you are capable of fulfilling it. P.141

BGO 37) You are expected to keep your promises, and so are they. P.142

BGO 38) Smacking is NOT an effective long term deterrent. P.142

BGO 39) You CAN apologise to your children and it doesn't hurt. P.145

BGO 40) It's OK to ask for help. P.151

BGO 41) SHE does still love you and she'll let you know once the children are in bed. If you're lucky. P.158

BGO 42) The odds are against both you and SHE being psychic you have to remember to keep communicating. P.161

BGO 43) Treasure your reputation and teach them to treasure theirs. P.182

BGO 44) There are no medals on Earth for getting the Difficult Questions right, but heaps of gongs for getting them wrong. P.184

BGO 45) You will never complete the task. Being a Dad is a job for life. P.190

Educating Daddy

Things a Dad Should Teach His Little People

Educate
How to kick, throw, pass and hit a ball.
How to tie shoelaces
How to fight with pretend swords
How to knot a tie
How to climb a tree
How to swim
How to do maths
How to look after your money
How to camp out properly in the wild
How to make a decent Gin and Tonic and pull a pint

Protect
How to throw a punch properly
How NOT to get in a fight
How to protect yourself if you do
How to protect girls
How to look after your brothers and sisters
How and when to call the police, fire service, doctor or ambulance

Provide (Capability and Activities)
How to use a hammer, screwdriver, spanner, and drill
How to put up a picture and a shelf
How to ride a bicycle and/or a scooter
How to mend a puncture and how to change a tyre
How to burn sausages on a Barbeque

Socialise
How to say Dad
How to say Please, Thank you and be polite
How to shake hands
How to look other people in the eye
How to be eat properly
How to open doors and give up seats for ladies
How to carry a bag or heavy load for a girl or lady
How to be kind
How to be nice to Mum
How to be good Dads and Mums themselves

Things Little People Think a Dad Should Know How to Do

Basic first aid

How to change a nappy

How to check the bath temperature for babies

How to make children go to sleep

Take children to sporting events (matches, tournaments)

How to cook basic meals (more than beans on toast)

How to iron

What School sports teams their children are in

What type of music their children like

Lots of Facts about the World and Life

Times tables

Spellings

Pronunciation

Card tricks and some magic

Basics about computers

Basics about business

How to make fire

How to use a mobile phone

Days of the week

Months in a year

About other ethnic groups

How to drive

Where the children are at night-time

What their children do at parties

How to do gardening/DIY

Know loads about sport

How to relax and play games with the children

Executive Summary

If you are one of those people who turn to the back of the book to see how it all ends without reading the intervening chapters, then the following 10 points (one for each finger) should satisfy you, but you have missed the logic and philosophy that underpins them in the previous pages. Don't be lazy, go back and read the words beforehand.

Daddy's Short Guide to Happy Children

The following ten points follow on from the Roles and Responsibilities of a father (see Chapter 3) as Provider, Protector, Law-maker and Educator. None of them are sacrosanct to Daddies and many are of course relevant to Mummies as well but, as with all within this book, they are the primary responsibility of the Father:

Safety and Security: No child should live in fear of its parents. You are your child's Protector even from yourself and its mother. Keep your cool and don't let them wind you up - you are the adult remember. Children grow best in a secure environment born out of the knowledge that they are wanted, loved and appreciated. They need a regular routine that sets times for meals, play and bedtime and standards for the levels of acceptable behaviour.

Feed, Clothe, Shelter, Educate: You made them, you provide for them. They are not a State responsibility, they are your responsibility and divorce, dislike or selfishness will not change your role or responsibility. There may come a time, 50 years hence, when the roles are reversed so, if you get the first part right, they might be prepared to get the second part right.

Praise and Reward: Children respond best to love, attention and praise. Take a Hedge Fund Manageris approach and invest heavily for future rewards. They cost nothing, so donit be mean in dishing them out ñ just donit get trapped into the falsehood of material rewards.

Example: You set the example that your children will follow. Children do as children see in every aspect, so expect your standards, behaviour, language, diet and habits to be mirrored by them. If you don't like them, then ask yourself where they got them from?

Boundaries: Children need to know where their boundaries are set and what is and is not acceptable. You are the Law-Maker, you set the law and let them know what you expect.

Consistency: The laws you set need to be consistently applied, to them, to their siblings, their friends and to yourself. Make sure that Mummy is in on the deal.

Graduated Discipline: Children are individuals not automatons. They will need firm and fair control with a recognizable set of warnings, ultimatums and penalties. Never make a rule you cannot or are not prepared to enforce.

Explain: Children need to be told what is expected of them. Don't reason with them or make it too complex, just tell them the obvious reasons for what you want and why you want it. Equally, when they go wrong, explain why and talk through the effects of their actions. Make sure that they understand where they went wrong and why they are going to be penalised.

Risk and Responsibility: Children need to grow up exploring their world and pushing the boundaries. They will grow in self-confidence and capability if you let them take reasonable risks and bear responsibility for their actions. Your job is to make sure they are safe and able to achieve what they set out to do.

Socialisation and Relaxation: Above all, the one thing that each of your children wants is your focussed attention and their own Precious Time with you. It doesn't matter when it happens but you need to plan and programme in a special time or a special activity that you spend with each of them in turn. Keeping yourself in good health is equally important and don't forget to plan in a block of free time for yourself, and your wife/partner as well to keep you balanced and sane.

Memo

To: Daddy
From: Your Child
SUBJECT: ME and YOU

Dear Daddy,

Please help me to love myself. I know quite well that I shouldn't get everything that I ask you for, I'm only really testing you – so don't spoil me. But do give me the rules and boundaries that I need and make sure I stay inside them.

Please help me feel good about myself by telling me about the good things you see in me more often that you tell me about the things you don't like. Don't ridicule me or imply that my inappropriate behaviour means that I am a bad person – I'm just trying to see how big the world really is!

Please be patient with me – I might be a late bloomer, and don't be too upset when I sometimes say 'I hate you'. It isn't you I hate, but your power over me.
Please don't shout or nag. If you do, I shall protect myself by appearing to be deaf. When YOU have a bad day, please don't take your frustrations out on me

Please don't bribe me or make rash promises. Remember that I feel badly let down when promises are broken, and don't be inconsistent - that completely confuses me and makes me lose faith in you.

Please listen to my worries and don't tell me that my fears are silly. They are terribly real to me and you can do so much to reassure me if you try to understand. The more you give me the safety to expose my true feelings, the more I will risk showing you my real self. (It's hidden in here somewhere.)

Please don't think it is beneath your dignity to apologize to me. An honest apology makes me feel surprisingly warm to wards you. I also need my sense of dignity, so please don't belittle me in front of other people. I'll take more notice if you talk to me with as much respect as you give to your best grown-up friends.

Please keep reminding me that I am basically a good and capable and worthwhile, so that I can grow up loving and accepting myself.

PS. I love you and Mummy and I don't expect you to be perfect either !

Further Reading from Bentwyck Henry Publishers

Books available from bookshops, Amazon.co.uk, or direct from the Publisher, Bentwyck Henry Publishers, 36 Hart Street, Henley-on-Thames, Oxon, RG9 2AU, email: bentwyckhenrybks@aol.com, www.bentwyckhenry.co.uk, 01491413100

Bruce Lee: Fighting Talk
Bruce Thomas

You may be Bruce Lee's No. 1 fan, or this may be your first encounter with him - either way you will find this book fascinating. Fighting Talk is a compilation of anecdotes, interviews and essays that were not included in the author's best selling full-length Bruce Lee biography.
ISBN 1904538-002, Paperback, £9.99

Caught! Prisoner of War No. 487
Dorrien Belson

Caught is the autobiography of a young Territorial Army Officer in World War II, who, like thousands of others, was captured near Dunkirk in 1940 during the first main battle of the war and spent 5 years in Prisoner-of War camps. Related with a dry humour, this true story is complemented with a wealth of historically interesting photographs and illustrations.
ISBN 1904538-010, Hardback b/w and colour illus, £14.99

On the Road...Again
Bruce Thomas

An autobiography written in the style of a novel. Bruce's first book, The big Wheel, written whilst touring with Elvis Costello and the Attractions, became a cult classic. On the Road...Again, describes a series of disturbing experiences starting with a mugging leading the author to Scotland, Arizona, and New Mexico - through the insights of kung fu, shamanism, Native American tradition, and remote viewing and to meetings with men and women with remarkable abilities.
ISBN 1904538-037, Hardback, £13.99

The Heir to Longbourn
Laurence Fleming

This elegant and entertaining piece of historical romance explores the question of the succession to Longbourn, the home in Pride and Prejudice of Mr and Mrs Bennet. The author ingeniously incorporates characters from four Jane Austen novels - Pride and Prejudice, Mansfield Park, Northanger Abbey and Persuasion
ISBN 1904538-053, Hardback £12.99